Powerful Habits for Overcoming Anxiety

Strategies for Inner Calm

FAIR WINDS

Contents

INTRODUCTIONS
The Powerful Habits Series • *6*
Introduction to This Book • *7*

PART ONE | **UNDERSTANDING AND OVERCOMING ANXIETY** • *9*

01 What Is Anxiety and What Causes It? • *10*
Some Anxiety Is Good, Too Much Is Bad • *12*
Symptoms of Anxiety Disorders • *14*
What's Your Anxiety Type? • *14*
› *Determine Your Anxiety Type* WORKSHEET • *17*
What Causes Anxiety Disorders? • *18*
› *What Are Your Anxiety Symptoms?* WORKSHEET • *21*
Assess the Severity of Your Symptoms • *22*
› *What Sensations Interfere with Your Life?* WORKSHEET • *22*
The Subjective Units of Distress Scale (SUDS) • *23*
› *Symptom Severity* WORKSHEET • *25*
How the Brain Works: Neuroplasticity and Learning New Habits • *26*
Turning Off the Fight-or-Flight Response: Learning Habits to Overcome Your Anxiety • *28*
Activate Your Left Frontal Lobe to Relieve Anxiety • *29*

PART TWO | **POWERFUL HABITS TO OVERCOME ANXIETY** • *31*

02 Change Your Dietary Habits to Tune Up Your Brain • *32*

Habit #1: Feed Your Brain Amino Acids • *34*

Eat Three Balanced Meals a Day • *36*

› *Balancing Your Meals* WORKSHEET • *37*

Habit #2: Eat Healthy Fats and Brain Boosting Nutrients • *38*

Vitamin C • *38*

Vitamin B • *39*

Drink Enough Water • *40*

Calcium, Magnesium, and Potassium • *41*

Five-Minute Habits • *43*

03 Fine-Tune Your Body • *44*

Habit #1: Learn to Breathe to Relax • *46*

Counteract Fight-of-Flight by Breathing the Right Way • *47*

Breathing Lessons • *48*

Habit #2: Stretch Away the Tension • *50*

Habit #3: Move Your Body to Relax • *52*

04 Cultivate Calm • *54*

Habit #1: Practice the Relaxation Response • *56*

The Seven Principles of Relaxation • *58*

Habit #2: Use Visualization to Achieve a Sense of Peace • *60*

Habit #3: Try Self-Hypnosis • *62*

Habit #4: Practice Meditation and Prayer • *64*

› *Relaxation Monitoring* WORKSHEET • *68*

05 Change Your Thinking to Change the Way You Feel · *70*

Habit #1: Use Reality Testing to Reduce Anxiety · *72*

Habit #2: Use Cognitive Restructuring to Reduce Anxiety · *74*

Habit #3: Verbally Relabel Experiences to Reduce Anxiety · *75*

Habit #4: Change Your Automatic Thoughts to Reduce Anxiety · *77*

› *New Automatic Thoughts* WORKSHEET · *81*

Habit #5: Adopt Anxiety-Reducing Assumptions · *82*

Habit #6: Restructure Your Negative (and Stressful) Core Beliefs · *84*

› *Refute Your Stressful Core Beliefs* WORKSHEET · *87*

› *New Core Beliefs* WORKSHEET · *88*

06 Facing Your Fears · *90*

Avoiding What You Fear Makes Anxiety Worse · *92*

› *Avoidance Questionnaire* WORKSHEET · *93*

Habit #1: Identify Your Escape, Avoidance, Procrastination, and Safety Behaviors · *96*

› *Escape Behavior Identifier* WORKSHEET · *97*

› *Avoidance Behavior Identifier* WORKSHEET · *98*

› *Procrastination Identifier* WORKSHEET · *99*

› *Safety Behavior Identifier* WORKSHEET · *100*

› *Avoidance Timeline* WORKSHEET · *101*

› *Fear Hierarchy Worksheet* WORKSHEET · *103*

Habit #2: Learn to Recondition Yourself · *104*

Habit #3: Practice Exposure and Observation · *107*

Habit #4: Practice Real-Life Exposure · *108*

› *In Vivo Exposure* WORKSHEET · *110*

Habit #5: Practice Increasing Your Exposure Intensity (Imagined and In Vivo) · *112*

› *SUDS Exposure* WORKSHEET · *113*

07 Accepting Your Bodily Sensations · 114
Learning to Not Fear Feeling · 116
Habit #1: Become More Comfortable in Your Body · 118
Habit #2: Desensitize Yourself to Bodily Sensations · 119
› *Assess Your Physical Sensations* WORKSHEET · 121
› *Identify Your Coping Skills* WORKSHEET · 122
Habit #3: Practice Your Coping Skills · 123
› *Over-Breathing* WORKSHEET · 126
› *Breath-Holding* WORKSHEET · 127
› *Body Tension* WORKSHEET · 128
› *Staring* WORKSHEET · 129
› *Shaking Your Head* WORKSHEET · 130
› *Head Between Your Legs* WORKSHEET · 131
Habit #4: Practice Interoceptive Exposure Whenever You Feel Anxious · 132

PART THREE | **MANAGING RELAPSES AND SETBACKS · 133**

08 Preventing Relapse · 134
Habit #1: Practice Good Self-Care · 136
Habit #2: Identify Your Anxiety Triggers · 138
› *Cues Planning* WORKSHEET · 140
Habit #3: Avoid Avoidance and Expose Yourself to Anxiety-Provoking Cues · 141
Habit #4: Learn How to Manage Setbacks without Overreacting · 142
› *How Do You Deal with Setbacks?* WORKSHEET · 144
Habit #5: Yes, You Can Get Back on Track After a Setback · 145
Habit #6: Learn to Practice Assertiveness · 146
Habit #7: Focus on Your Weakest Skill to Make All of You Strong · 148
Habit #8: Create Your Relapse-Prevention Plan · 153
› *Relapse-Prevention Monitoring* WORKSHEET · 154

INDEX · 156

THE POWERFUL HABITS SERIES

habit /hăb·ĭt/ noun

1. A recurrent, often unconscious pattern of behavior that is acquired through frequent repetition.
2. An established disposition of the mind or character.
3. Customary manner or practice.

   The American Heritage® Dictionary of the English Language, 5th Edition

What Can You Achieve in Five Minutes?

Plenty. **Powerful Habits** is a new series that focuses on practical, immediately applicable strategies that can uplevel your health and life starting today. Instead of wading through hundreds of pages, numerous steps, and a complicated program, *Powerful Habits* gives you quick-take advice, much of which can be done in five minutes or less.

Your habits can define who you are. But much of your behavior is unconscious and bad habits have a way of taking root without us noticing it. The good news? You can counteract this by making good habits a part of your day and your life. It's like putting money in the bank. If you do it consistently, you'll build wealth through your actions and the interest that accumulates.

It's the same way with adopting habits to help you reduce and overcome your anxiety. For example, say you begin to practice the habit of diaphragmatic breathing whenever you feel anxious. Breathing deeply, especially with a longer exhalation, will help you relax. You'll shift from the fight-or-flight response (activated by your sympathetic nervous system) to the relaxation response (activated by your parasympathetic nervous system) and feel less anxious.

Over time, when you feel anxious, you'll habitually return to breathing this way, which will help you feel calm. This will give you the clarity to adopt more of the habits in this book to overcome your anxiety. It's a win-win!

Inside this book, you'll find new habits that you can read and put into practice in just a few minutes each day and see results in real-time. Open the book, discover a new habit, and apply the advice to your life. Your better self is five minutes away!

Introduction to This Book

If you are plagued by anxiety, you are not alone. Anxiety disorders are more common in the United States than any other psychological problem, including depression. Some estimates indicate that 301 million people around the world have an anxiety disorder. In the United States, 1 in 3 adults do.

We live in a stress-filled world. Terrorism, pandemics, financial and job pressures, and wars around the globe have all contributed to an underlying sense of anxiety in our day-to-day lives. Although most of us find ways to deal with that anxiety, some people experience it in the extreme and can, as a result, develop anxiety disorders.

Living with an anxiety disorder can be a challenge. It can make getting through the day and enjoying your life difficult. An anxiety disorder can put your life in *dis*order.

The good news is that you can bring your anxiety disorder under control. Just as your body has the ability to heal wounds, so can your brain. Your brain has the capacity to change through a process known as *neuroplasticity,* which means rewiring your brain. This book will help you discover how to do just that. It contains habits you can cultivate to feel better. You'll learn:

- *How anxiety develops*

- *The types of anxiety*

- *How your brain works and how to rewire it*

- *What you can do to make your brain more capable of rewiring*

- *Which foods and nutritional supplements create the right biochemistry to help your brain make you calmer*

- *How to restructure your thinking, so that you can make your anxiety work for you, instead of against you*

- *How to avoid avoidance and maximize exposure, and how to keep from overreacting to the physical sensations associated with anxiety*

- *How to prevent relapse*

In the following chapters, you'll discover the practices that can help you overcome panic disorder, phobia, and generalized anxiety. These practices are called "brain-based" and "evidence-based." Brain-based practices help you change how you think. Because your brain is central to everything you do and feel, when you rewire your brain, you can put anxiety behind you.

Evidence-based practices are techniques that are known to help overcome anxiety. After performing hundreds of studies on treating anxiety disorders, psychologists have found that some techniques work and some do not. You are going to learn the ones that work. In this book, you'll discover how to heal your anxiety from a *biopsychosocial* perspective—that is, biologically, psychologically, and socially.

A biopsychosocial approach is comprehensive because anxiety encompasses biological (your brain and the rest of your body), psychological (thinking and feeling), and social (social and cultural contexts) aspects.

By following the practices in this book, you can physically change your brain and body, change the way you think to help you change the way you feel, and change the way you approach social situations. You'll learn how to rewire your brain and alter the way your body functions. You'll learn to restructure your thoughts, so that your emotions can follow their lead. You'll also learn to use the social world around you to enhance your comfort level.

What this book will *not* cover is the use of medications to treat anxiety disorders. That's because most people can heal their anxiety without them. Anti-anxiety medications, such as Ativan and Valium, can impede your ability to heal your anxiety in the long term and can contribute to a range of negative side effects, such as depression, sleep problems, and addiction. Selective serotonin reuptake inhibitors (SSRIs), such as Paxil and Prozac, have been found to have anti-anxiety effects, but they also come with side effects. If you want your gains to be permanent, don't rely on medications. They are only useful when you use them. Try the methods described in this book before considering medications.

Finally, this is not just a book *about* anxiety. It is a book on *how to heal* your anxiety. As you read through it, you'll learn how to overcome excessive anxiety, and you'll practice methods to overcome it through a series of exercises. With practice and the techniques you learn in the book, you, too, can live a life free of anxiety disorders.

Part One

Understanding and Overcoming Anxiety

Anxiety can be a difficult thing to live with. One minute you're feeling fine, the next you're on edge, tense, and stressed. Although some anxiety is normal, especially in the world we live in, too much—being hypervigilant and feeling stressed out every day—can wear you down. Overcoming anxiety begins with understanding why it happens, what the symptoms and causes of anxiety disorders are and what exactly is going on in your brain and nervous system to cause it. You'll learn about all these aspects of anxiety and more in Part One. Read on to find out more.

What Is Anxiety and What Causes It?

01

How much do you know about anxiety, what causes it, and how the brain is involved?

Take this quiz to find out >

TRUE

FALSE

T F *Some anxiety can be a good thing.*

T F *If you have an anxiety disorder, you'll experience all of its symptoms.*

T F *Symptom clusters can help define the disorders you may have.*

T F *The causes of anxiety can be unique.*

T F *There's no reliable way to measure the severity of your anxiety.*

T F *Neuroplasticity enables your brain to adopt new habits that reduce anxiety.*

T F *Activating your right frontal lobe means a calmer you.*

You'll find the answers in this chapter.

Some Anxiety Is Good... Too Much Is Bad

Some anxiety can be a good thing.
TRUE

Everyone experiences anxiety once in a while—when the car breaks down on the way to a job interview, for example, or when you're standing on the high-diving board and the water looks a *long* way down. Anxiety is a fact of life. In fact, *some* anxiety is necessary. You need a little anxiety to get to work on time or to get to the grocery store before it closes. If you didn't have anxiety, you wouldn't know to get out of the way when you see a truck bearing down on you in the street.

Anxiety can be a bad thing, however, if you worry that your boss doesn't like you, even though you have no realistic evidence that he does not, or if you feel panic when there are "too many" people in the grocery store, or if you avoid crossing streets, because you never know when a truck is going to come out of nowhere. Anxiety becomes a problem when it gets turned on too high.

Feeling constant tension and worry makes each day trying at best and a walking nightmare at worst. And when you're extremely fearful about a situation—meeting new people, for instance—your life becomes severely limited. You can feel like you're walking through a minefield when you're plagued by panic attacks, because you never know when one might occur. When anxiety becomes extreme, it's considered an anxiety disorder. But an anxiety disorder doesn't have to be permanent.

HOW JAKE AND TOM EXPERIENCE ANXIETY

Jake and Tom were both scheduled to take a seminar on a new computer program. Jake was excited about the opportunity to get out of the office and meet new people. Although he was a little anxious about whether he was going to be able to learn the entire system, he was eager to give it a try.

Tom was reluctant to go to the seminar. He tried to get out of it by saying he had too much work to do at the office. Secretly, he feared having to meet new people and was particularly afraid of being asked to speak. He even thought of quitting his job, so that he would not have to go to the seminar, but decided against it because it would mean going to job interviews, which he feared more than the seminar.

As Tom drove to the building in which the seminar was being held, his heart began to pound, his breathing became shallow, and he started sweating profusely. As he stepped out of the car, his thoughts raced by so fast, he couldn't decide what to do. Should he go to the hospital, or should he sit back down in his car and hope this nightmare didn't kill him? When Jake arrived, he anxiously looked Tom over and asked, "Are you okay? Should I call the paramedics?" Tom nodded yes.

Jake dialed 911, then anxiously turned to Tom. "Is it your heart?" Tom looked horrified and again nodded yes. Jake paced nervously, hoping that the ambulance would arrive before Tom died.

Which of these two men had anxiety? Both did. But Jake's anxiety was adaptive. It helped him spring into action to help a man in distress. Tom's anxiety was maladaptive. In fact, he was having a panic attack.

Tom's anxiety was a problem, because he became paralyzed by it. Tom is an example of someone with an anxiety disorder.

Symptoms of Anxiety Disorders

If you have an anxiety disorder, you'll experience all of its symptoms.

FALSE

You might not experience all the symptoms common to a specific disorder, and you might find that some of your symptoms fall into more than one category. This is because anxiety affects people in different ways. Below is a list of many of the most common anxiety disorders and the symptoms for each one.

What's Your Anxiety Type?

Generalized anxiety disorder (GAD)

If you suffer from GAD, you tend to worry excessively about your future, health, family, friends, and safety. You also probably feel tense and anxious much of the time. You might think of yourself as a chronic worrier and can torture yourself with "what-if" thoughts throughout the day that cause more anxiety. GAD differs from PD and phobias because the anxiety is like chronic pain. Although the free-floating anxiety and worry are not intense, they seem to be there all the time and can worsen depending on the situation.

- **Worrying much of the time**
- **Muscle tension**
- **Irritability**
- **Restlessness, feeling keyed up**
- **Difficulty concentrating**
- **Mind going blank**
- **Easily fatigued**

Panic disorder (PD)

PD includes panic attacks. They're triggered by a false alarm: you believe that the sensations you are experiencing are real and this triggers the *fight-or-flight response,* a physiological response to a threat. It is inherited from your ancestors, who were often confronted with life-threatening situations.

Today, you may experience these symptoms if you're stressed out at work because you can't meet a deadline. You can react to these symptoms in two ways: You can see them for what they are—a physical reaction to stress—or you can consider them an alarm for something more ominous, such as a heart attack. When you overreact to those symptoms, you can tumble into a panic attack.

- **Unsteadiness**
- **Feelings of terror**
- **Nervousness**
- **Feelings of choking**
- **Trembling hands**
- **Shakiness**
- **Fear of losing control**
- **Difficulty breathing**
- **Indigestion or nausea**
- **Feeling faint**

- **Flushed face**
- **Cold sweat**
- **Wobbliness in legs**
- **Feeling hot**
- **Dizziness or light-headedness**
- **Numbness or tingling**
- **Fear of the worst happening**
- **Inability to relax**
- **Pounding or racing heart**

PANIC DISORDER AND DEPRESSION

PD can occur with other anxiety disorders. As many as 50 percent of people with PD have GAD, phobias, and obsessive-compulsive disorder (OCD), as well as disorders such as depression. If you have PD and also suffer from depression, this can complicate your efforts to overcome panic disorder. For these reasons, you should get help with your depression before or simultaneously with learning how to heal your anxiety.

> **WHAT'S SOCIAL ANXIETY DISORDER (SAD)?**
>
> SAD is a type of social anxiety where you have a marked and persistent fear of particular social situations that expose you to unfamiliar people or to possible scrutiny by others. You fear that you'll be seen as anxious or act in a way that will be humiliating or embarrassing. You may feel overwhelmed and even experience a panic attack. Your impulse is to avoid situations that trigger SAD. Some people feel anxious around authority figures like police officers or in groups.

Phobias

Phobias are connected to a specific type of stress trigger. You experience an intense fear of specific objects, situations, or environments.

- **Intense fear cued by the presence or anticipation of a specific object or situation (for example, heights, enclosed spaces, crowds, or flying)**
- **Marked feelings of anxiety when encountering that object or situation**
- **Extreme avoidance of that object or situation**

Social phobia

If you experience anxiety in situations such as meeting new people or being in a room with strangers and go out of your way to avoid these situations, you likely suffer from a social phobia.

- **Fear of failure**
- **Fear of social ridicule**
- **Fear of rejection**
- **Stage fright**
- **Intense fear of talking to strangers**

***Symptom clusters can help define
the disorders you may have.***

TRUE

People who suffer from anxiety often experience distress in the form
of symptom *clusters*. These clusters indicate a particular type of
anxiety disorder. For example, a cluster of symptoms that includes
rapid heartbeat, shortness of breath, and sweating occurring together
represents PD. Write your symptom clusters down below. This will
help you identify your type of anxiety disorder.

Determine Your Anxiety Type WORKSHEET

What Are Your Symptom Clusters?

What Causes Anxiety Disorders?

The causes of anxiety can be unique.
TRUE

There are actually many causes of excessive anxiety. And what causes *your* anxiety may not be the same as what causes another person's anxiety, even if you both have the same type of anxiety disorder.

Biological, Psychological, and Social Factors

You can become vulnerable to developing anxiety disorders because of a variety of biological, psychological, and social factors. These factors make up your biopsychosocial experience.

Biological factors include genetics and neurochemistry, such as a family history of anxiety disorders. Brain-based conditioning and psychological factors involve your early attachment relationship with your parents and the quality of your relationships with your family members. For example, if your parents made you feel anxious, rather than comforted, around them, you can be prone to anxiety.

Psychological factors also include your cognitive skills. If you think in black-and-white terms or hold yourself to extreme perfectionist standards, you're likely to experience anxiety.

Social factors include how well you adjust to your culture, ethnicity, and social situations, such as work, social gatherings, and cultural expectations. These factors comprise who you are and how you adapt to the world. None of them act independently.

ADJUSTMENT DISORDER WITH ANXIETY

If you have recently experienced a great deal of stress associated with a major life event, such as a divorce, taking on a challenging new job, or moving, you may experience a surge of anxiety with symptoms similar to GAD and even have panic attacks. This is a reaction to an out-of-the-ordinary stressor.

Often the anxiety goes away when the stressor goes away. If it persists—maybe you continue to avoid situations and experiences that make you anxious—it can develop into an anxiety disorder. Using the exercises and techniques in this book can help alleviate your anxiety, even if it doesn't develop into a major disorder. They can also help you cope with your stressors until they pass.

Each dimension of your biopsychosocial experience overlaps the others:

The biological aspect involves your physical sensations, such as when you experience a rapid heartbeat or sweating. If you misinterpret these physical sensations as cause for alarm, you tend to increase your anxiety and might even experience a panic attack, leading you to believe that you are having a heart attack. The result is that you become extremely fearful of those physical sensations, doing everything you can to avoid them in the future.

Or perhaps your palms sweat and your voice quivers a little when you meet new people. Becoming extremely concerned that someone might notice stirs up more anxiety, which contributes to an increase in sweaty palms and your voice quivering.

The psychological aspect of your biopsychosocial experience involves what you say to yourself when you experience anxiety. If you are a pessimist, a black-and-white thinker, or tend to catastrophize if things don't go perfectly, you'll stir up more anxiety. For example, say you encounter an unanticipated snag in your effort to complete a project. You could be flexible and roll with the bumps on the road, or you could say to yourself, "Everything's falling apart! Now what am I going to do?" Your pessimism and inflexibility set you up to see a bump as more than a bump—it's an impassable boulder in the road, a catastrophe.

Your "mood state" also affects how you think about and interpret the events in your life. When you're in particular mood, your thoughts can be colored by that mood. You make statements to yourself about what you are experiencing at any given moment, and if those statements are colored by an anxious state of mind, they can perpetuate anxiety.

The social aspect of the biopsychosocial experience involves a fear that other people will see that you have an anxiety disorder, which can affect your relationship with them. If you are with people you don't know, for example, you might say to yourself, "What if he can tell that I'm nervous? He'll think I'm an idiot." Statements like these heighten your anxiety.

It's important to understand that you can heal your anxiety without knowing what caused it. You don't need to discover the initial cause of the anxiety before you can take steps to dissolve it. Here are some specific causes of anxiety disorder.

Do you see yourself here?

- Genetics, inheriting an anxious or shy temperament
- Growing up with anxious parents who model their anxiety and worry about everything
- Poor attachment relationships with your parents or caregivers, making it hard for you to feel connected and comforted by other people
- Being criticized consistently while growing up, causing you to be overcritical of yourself
- Experiencing physical, sexual, or emotional abuse, which can cause you to feel undeserving of the good things in life
- Traumatic experiences that have a lingering effect by making you hypervigilant for similar trauma
- Side effects of medical problems, including mitral valve prolapse, exposure to toxins, and mediations, including monoamine oxidase inhibitors, calcium channel blockers, and theophylline, and over-the-counter medications, such as antihistamines, which can also mimic anxiety symptoms
- Embracing thinking styles, such as perfectionism and black-and-white thinking, that decrease your flexibility and adaptability
- Creating biochemistry that stirs anxiety through poor eating habits
- Trying to avoid feeling any kind of stress

What Are Your Anxiety Symptoms? WORKSHEET

To determine to what degree you're troubled by anxiety, it will be helpful to identify your symptoms. You can refer back to this list as you adopt some of the habits in this book. Check off the symptoms that apply to you:

- ○ Numbness or tingling
- ○ Feeling hot
- ○ Wobbliness in legs
- ○ Inability to relax
- ○ Fear of the worst happening
- ○ Dizziness or lightheadedness
- ○ Pounding or racing heart
- ○ Unsteadiness
- ○ Feeling terrified
- ○ Nervousness
- ○ Feelings of choking
- ○ Trembling hands
- ○ Shakiness
- ○ Fear of losing control

- ○ Difficulty breathing
- ○ Fear of dying
- ○ Indigestion or nausea
- ○ Feeling faint
- ○ Flushed face
- ○ Cold sweat
- ○ Worrying much of the time
- ○ Muscle tension
- ○ Restlessness, feeling keyed up
- ○ Irritability
- ○ Difficulty concentrating
- ○ Mind going blank
- ○ Easily fatigued
- ○ Fear of failure
- ○ Fear of rejection
- ○ Fear of social ridicule

The more symptoms you checked off, the greater the role anxiety plays in your life. You might experience symptoms that are not on the list. Write them down in the space below.

....

....

....

....

....

....

Assess the Severity of Your Symptoms

The next question to ask yourself is whether your symptoms have been increasing in severity. In general, the more severe your anxiety symptoms, the more they negatively impact your life. Often, the severity of the symptoms increases over time. This can happen if you make efforts to *avoid* the situations that make you anxious. If your anxiety is severe, it can start to impinge on your life.

What Sensations Interfere with Your Life? WORKSHEET

> **CYNTHIA'S WORLD SHRINKS**
>
> Cynthia, a graduate student in history, was afraid of driving on the freeway. She started to panic whenever she was in a car on the freeway, so she started to avoid them. Sometimes she added hours to her commute to avoid the freeways. Soon, she was feeling anxious about driving in general. Even driving on the city streets made her anxious.
>
> Cynthia decided that she would retreat to her comfort level, so that she could regroup to gather her strength. Once she "felt ready again," she would drive again, not only on the city streets but also on the freeways.
>
> As time went on, however, Cynthia grew to feel *more*, not less, anxious about driving. She felt like she was falling into quicksand, sinking day by day into feeling anxious all the time. One day, she told her husband, who was becoming frustrated because he had become her taxi service, that she felt she was "having a mental breakdown."
>
> Cynthia's anxiety about driving on the freeways was interfering with her life.
>
> In the worksheet on the opposite page, write down the sensations that interfere with your life and keep you from doing the things you want and need to do.
>
> By identifying these sensations, you will be in a better position to confront and neutralize them in the exercises that follow. The end result will be that they won't stand in the way of you enjoying your life.
>
>

The Subjective Units of Distress Scale (SUDS)

There's no reliable way to measure the severity of your anxiety.

FALSE

The *Subjective Units of Distress Scale,* or **SUDS,** is a method of measuring the severity of your anxiety. It will help you target the anxiety situations that need to be addressed and to gauge your progress. The information can also help you figure out whether you *are* suffering from an anxiety disorder and, if so, what type of disorder you have.

THE SUBJECTIVE UNITS OF DISTRESS SCALE

RATING	SEVERITY	DESCRIPTION
0	None	You feel no distress or anxiety. You are absolutely calm and relaxed.
10	Minimal	You feel mostly calm, but have a twinge of tension or alertness that isn't very noticeable.
20	Mild	You feel slightly tense or nervous, but are still able to focus on your work or social activities.
30	Mild	You feel mildly stressed, tense, or nervous. You can work or socialize, but you have to actively manage the anxiety in some way, and you might be irritable. Your body may be tense or "keyed up."
40	Moderate	You feel mild-to-moderate anxiety, and are somewhat distracted or irritable. You have mild physical symptoms, such as muscle tension, shakiness, or feeling weak.
50	Moderate	You are moderately anxious or stressed, and it is interfering somewhat with your ability to focus or work. You are distracted, hyperalert, and on your guard. Physical symptoms can include increased heart rate, lightheadedness, butterflies, and irregular breathing.
60	Moderate	You are very anxious, distracted, and hypervigilant. You might feel dizzy, lightheaded, or shaky, with a rapid heart rate, tightness in the chest, and nausea.
70	Severe	You are intensely anxious or stressed, with strong physical symptoms. You are having difficulty concentrating on anything but the anxiety.
80	Severe	Your anxiety is very intense and overwhelming, with significant physical symptoms (pounding heart, rapid breathing, sweating, dizziness, nausea). You are focused on wanting to get out of the situation.
90	Extreme	You are in a state of extreme fear and distress and are having difficulty coping. Physical sensations are intense, and you are entirely focused on escaping the situation.
100	Extreme	You are in full panic mode and fear you may die, faint, or lose your mind. Your fear is so intense that you are overwhelmed and can only think of escape.

Symptom Severity WORKSHEET

In the chart below, write your symptoms and their SUDS, starting with the most severe.

SYMPTOMS	SUDS

How the Brain Works: Neuroplasticity and Learning New Habits

Neuroplasticity enables your brain to adopt new habits that reduce anxiety.
TRUE

Although your brain weighs only three pounds, it contains 100 billion nerve cells, called neurons, and many more support cells. More powerful than any computer, your brain is not hardwired—it can create or reduce anxiety, according to what you do and how you think.

Your neurons have the ability to make new connections with one another. Those connections change as you learn things, such as how to become relaxed, instead of anxious. Your neurons communicate by sending chemical messengers called "neurotransmitters" to one another across a gap called a "synapse." This transmission is how one neuron gets another neuron to fire. You have more than one hundred types of neurotransmitters in your brain. Some, such as epinephrine, make you anxious, and some, including gamma-aminobutyric acid (GABA) and serotonin, calm you down. You want the neurotransmitters GABA and serotonin to work more efficiently in your brain, because they promote calmness and a better mood.

The synapses between your neurons also can change to make you less anxious. This ability to change is called "neuroplasticity." Neuroplasticity makes learning new habits possible. Your brain changes its synapses when you learn something new, including how to be calmer.

Cells That Fire Together, Wire Together

The phrase "cells that fire together, wire together" describes how your brain reorganizes itself through neuroplasticity as you learn new things. The more frequently the new connections between your neurons fire together, the higher the chance they will fire together in the future and produce calmness instead of nervousness.

They are "wired together" because you are strengthening these new connections. This is the brain-based explanation for how habits get formed and how you can alternatively modify those habits. The more you practice something, the more likely you are to do it in the future. In other words, the more you practice feeling relaxed, the more likely you are to feel relaxed in general. The same process applies to the anxiety techniques in this book. Neuroplasticity occurs when you do something over and over again. In other words, repetition rewires your brain and creates habits.

However, creating new habits requires effort. When water runs downhill, for example, it's following the path of least resistance. Your brain does this, too—it does what it is used to doing. If you want to

THE ANATOMY OF YOUR BRAIN

Learning how your brain and body work can give you a tangible understanding of your anxiety disorder and a sense of hope that you can gain mastery over it. Your brain contains:

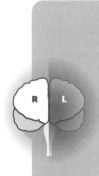

Hemispheres Your right hemisphere is talented at getting the "big picture," or gist, of a situation. It is generally more creative and activates when you learn something new. Once you learn a skill, it often is encoded in your left hemisphere, where routines, linear sequencing, and language are processed. Your right hemisphere processes negative emotions, and your left hemisphere processes positive emotions.

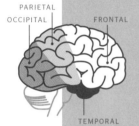

Lobes Each of your two hemispheres has four major parts, called "lobes." In each set of lobes are primary areas that are specialized for certain skills. For example, your occipital lobes specialize in vision; your temporal lobes in hearing, memory, and recognition; the parietal lobes in sensing physical sensation; and your frontal lobes in movement, problem-solving, and initiating behaviors.

Your Frontal Lobes A sort of brain within the brain, your frontal lobes are sometimes called the "executive brain" and decide what to do, how to stay positive, and how to appreciate the larger picture of life. Your left frontal lobe is associated with positive feelings and action, and your right frontal lobe is associated with negative (anxious) feelings and withdrawal.

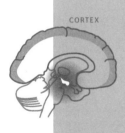

The Cerebral Cortex The outer surface of your two hemispheres is called the "cortex," or gray matter. Below cortex is "white matter," which consists of support cells covering the long nerve fibers that connect various parts of your brain.

The Amygdala and Hippocampus The amygdala, from *amygdalon*, the Latin word for "almond," is the threat detector and tends to be hypersensitive in people with anxiety disorders. Your amygdala triggers the fight-or-flight response via your hypothalamus-pituitary-adrenal axis (HPA). The hippocampus, named for its seahorse shape, helps you remember what is—and what is not—worthy of fear.

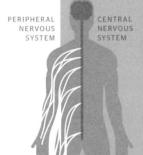

Peripheral Nervous System Consists of the voluntary (also called the "somatic") and the involuntary (also called the "autonomic"). Your autonomic nervous system can get activated, or it can calm down. It can turn off the fight-or-flight mode when you don't need it on. It has two branches: the sympathetic nervous system, which regulates arousal, and the parasympathetic nervous system, which regulates relaxation.

Your sympathetic branch activates your brain and body with neurotransmitters such as norepinephrine and epinephrine (adrenaline). The parasympathetic branch helps you calm down by releasing the brain neurotransmitter GABA, which acts to dampen the effects of adrenaline and to calm down your amygdala.

create a new habit, one your brain isn't familiar with, you need to make a strong effort to *do what you don't feel like doing*—and then keep doing it. Eventually, you'll find yourself doing it without the effort. It will have become a habit.

In other words, if you practice feeling relaxed, instead of feeling anxious, you'll feel relaxed more often than anxious. Likewise, if you practice putting yourself in situations that once triggered anxiety, you will eventually respond to them without anxiety. This is possible because you can decide to override the overactivity of your amygdala. The more you practice the techniques in this book, the calmer you'll be. Here are a few critical points that are important to remember:

- *Your brain is a complex organ that can change through neuroplasticity.*

- *If you continue to do what comes easily for you, your anxiety will continue.*

- *To conquer anxiety, you need to do what you don't feel like doing.*

- *Because your implicit memory systems and your amygdala can't change immediately, you need to repeat the skills that you learn in the book over and over again to establish new habits.*

Turning Off the Fight-or-Flight Response: Learning Habits to Overcome Your Anxiety

At the first sign of danger, the amygdala signals your hypothalamus to secrete a substance called cortical-releasing factor (CRF), which alerts your pituitary gland to release adrenocorticotropic hormone (ACTH) into your bloodstream. ACTH triggers your adrenal glands to release epinephrine and norepinephrine, two types of brain chemicals called "neurotransmitters." They charge up your sympathetic nervous system.

If stress persists, a stress hormone called "cortisol" is released to keep you activated. Cortisol further excites your amygdala. This activation system makes evolutionary sense, because if our ancestors encountered danger in specific situations, like saber-toothed tigers, they needed to act, but today, it can make us miserable. Once it gets turned on, it's hard to turn it off.

Activate Your Left Frontal Lobe to Relieve Anxiety

Activating your right frontal lobe means a calmer you.
FALSE

To conquer anxiety, you need to activate your left frontal lobe. Because your left frontal lobe has language skills that your right frontal lobe does not, it makes labeling sensations with words ("this is nothing to be worried about") an important part of overcoming anxiety. Its language ability allows you to label your experiences realistically, while activating your left frontal lobe and the positive emotions associated with it.

Your left frontal lobe and your orbital frontal cortex can shut down the HPA axis and the fight-or-flight response. This happens when you activate your left frontal lobe by from a realistic perspective, and then doing something positive. In other words, you label a false alarm for what it is—nothing to worry about—then you go ahead and expose yourself to the thing you feared, such as crossing a bridge or talking to strangers. Using this system, you can learn to tame your amygdala. That's what the rest of this book is all about: cultivating and practicing habits that can help you overcome your anxiety.

Part Two

Powerful Habits to Overcome Anxiety

Now that you've learned about the symptoms, causes, and types of anxiety, and the way your brain works, it's time to take action. In Part Two, you'll learn about powerful habits that you can use to change your eating habits to improve brain function, to change the way you breathe, stretch and move your body to relax, and to cultivate calm with effective practices like yoga and meditation. But that's not all. You'll learn how to change your negative thoughts—along with negative assumptions and negative core beliefs—to change the way you feel, which will help you defuse anxiety before it becomes overwhelming. By shifting to the present moment and identifying your escape, avoidance, procrastination, and safety behaviors, you'll also learn how to face your fears in real-life. Finally, you'll discover ways to accept and desensitize yourself from anxiety and learn new coping skills. Let's get started!

02
Change Your Dietary Habits to Tune Up Your Brain

How much do you really know about the connection between your anxiety and what you eat?

Take this quiz to find out >

TRUE

FALSE

(T) (F) *What you eat can determine whether you feel good or bad, calm or anxious.*

(T) (F) *Eating carb-rich meals is the best way to control anxiety.*

(T) (F) *All fats are bad for your brain.*

(T) (F) *A vitamin C deficiency can make you more stressed out.*

(T) (F) *A vitamin B deficiency can make you nervous and irritable.*

(T) (F) *There's no connection between drinking enough water and whether you feel anxious.*

(T) (F) *Eating foods high in calcium and magnesium help you remain calm.*

Read on to find the correct answers and you'll learn healthy habits to optimize brain function, ease anxiety and feel more calm.

HABIT #1
Feed Your Brain Amino Acids

What you eat can determine whether you feel good or bad, calm or anxious.
TRUE

What you eat affects your biochemistry, how your brain functions, and how you feel.

Your brain is the highest energy consumer of any organ in your body, and changes in your diet can have a major impact on its ability to function properly. What you eat can either calm you down or make you feel nervous.

The standard American diet can derail your efforts to reduce anxiety. You might crave sweet, salty comfort foods when you're stressed but this is counterproductive. Not only do sugary foods and caffeine rev you up, but like processed foods, they're missing the necessary vitamins, minerals, and other nutrients that provide the amino acids your body needs to stay calm.

Why Amino Acids Are So Important

The amino acids found in various foods are crucial building blocks for your brain's neurotransmitters. Your body manufactures these neurotransmitters by synthesizing specific amino acids in the foods you eat. For example, L-glutamine is an amino acid found in foods such as almonds and peaches, and when digested, your body uses it to synthesize the neurotransmitter GABA. GABA helps you stay calm. Protein contains amino acids that produce neurotransmitters, like serotonin and dopamine, and GABA too.

A Healthy Gut Produces Neurotransmitters You Need

In a healthy microbiome, which is a community of microorganisms in the gut, friendly bacteria produce neurotransmitters like serotonin, dopamine, and GABA. But sugars and chemicals from processed foods and a lack of nutrients interfere with this process because friendly bacteria don't have the right raw materials to work with.

This affects the way the gut, your second brain or enteric nervous system, talks to the brain through the gut-brain axis, which affects how you feel. In fact, a 2023 study in *Translational Psychiatry* showed that the gut composition of participants with SAD differed from the healthy control group.

Symptoms such as cramping, bloating, or constipation can indicate that your gut (and your brain) may be out of sync. Fermented foods can heal the gut because they contribute to a healthy gut microbiome. This, in turn, improves brain health. To help your gut heal:

- *Choose probiotic rich foods such as: plain yogurt, kefir, sauerkraut, pickles, kimchi, and fermented vegetables.*

- *Choose prebiotic-rich foods: onions, leeks, garlic, artichokes, asparagus, konjac, sunchokes, and apples.*

- *Fiber in foods like plants, vegetables, fruits, and grains also helps to maintain a healthy gut microbiome.*

Now that you know why neurotransmitters are so important, let's take a look at the chart that lists amino acid precursors, their associated neurotransmitters, and a sample of the foods that contain them.

AMINO ACIDS AND SOME FOODS THAT CONTAIN THEM

AMINO ACID PRECURSOR	NEUROTRANSMITTER	EFFECTS
L-tryptophan	**Serotonin**	**Improves sleep, calmness, and mood**
Turkey • Milk • Shredded wheat • Almonds • Pumpkin seeds • Cottage cheese • Soybeans		
L-glutamine	**GABA**	**Decreases tension and irritability; increases calmness**
Eggs • Peaches • Grape juice • Avocado • Sunflower oils/seeds • Granola • Peas		
Tyrosine	**Dopamine**	**Increases feelings of pleasure**
Beef • Fish • Oats • Wheat • Dairy products • Chicken • Soybeans		
L-phenylalanine	**Norepinephrine**	**Increases energy and feelings of pleasure; aids memory**
Peanuts • Lima beans • Sesame seeds • Chicken • Yogurt • Milk • Soybeans		

Eat Three Balanced Meals a Day

Eating carb-rich meals is the best way to control anxiety.
FALSE

A balanced meal ensures you consume anti-anxiety amino acids.

A turkey sandwich on whole wheat bread with carrots and a piece of fruit is a balanced meal. So is rice, fish, and a salad. A bowl of cereal with milk and strawberries is also a balanced meal. You can put many combinations together to create a balanced meal. Each meal should contain:

- *Protein (whether from animals or plants, such as soy)*
- *Fruit or vegetables*
- *Complex carbohydrates (such as whole grains, which can boost serotonin levels)*

GO MEDITERRANEAN!

The Mediterranean diet can be a good way to feed the brain (and gut) the right nutrients so that it can produce neurotransmitters and regulate mood. This way of eating focuses on vegetables, fruits, nuts, legumes, wild-caught fish like salmon, lean protein, and healthy fats (like extra-virgin olive oil), fiber, and whole grains.

Balancing Your Meals WORKSHEET

Use this worksheet to chart your progress. Simply check the box for each balanced meal you eat.

	BREAKFAST	LUNCH	DINNER
Su	○ PROTEIN ○ FRUIT/VEG ○ CARB	○ PROTEIN ○ FRUIT/VEG ○ CARB	○ PROTEIN ○ FRUIT/VEG ○ CARB
Mo	○ PROTEIN ○ FRUIT/VEG ○ CARB	○ PROTEIN ○ FRUIT/VEG ○ CARB	○ PROTEIN ○ FRUIT/VEG ○ CARB
Tu	○ PROTEIN ○ FRUIT/VEG ○ CARB	○ PROTEIN ○ FRUIT/VEG ○ CARB	○ PROTEIN ○ FRUIT/VEG ○ CARB
We	○ PROTEIN ○ FRUIT/VEG ○ CARB	○ PROTEIN ○ FRUIT/VEG ○ CARB	○ PROTEIN ○ FRUIT/VEG ○ CARB
Th	○ PROTEIN ○ FRUIT/VEG ○ CARB	○ PROTEIN ○ FRUIT/VEG ○ CARB	○ PROTEIN ○ FRUIT/VEG ○ CARB
Fr	○ PROTEIN ○ FRUIT/VEG ○ CARB	○ PROTEIN ○ FRUIT/VEG ○ CARB	○ PROTEIN ○ FRUIT/VEG ○ CARB
Sa	○ PROTEIN ○ FRUIT/VEG ○ CARB	○ PROTEIN ○ FRUIT/VEG ○ CARB	○ PROTEIN ○ FRUIT/VEG ○ CARB

HABIT #2
Eat Healthy Fats and Brain Boosting Nutrients

All fats are bad for your brain.
FALSE

Omega-3 fatty acids are critical for healthy cells (including brain cells).

Fat Head

Your brain is over 60 percent fat, so it needs healthy fats to function. However, your body does not manufacture these essential fatty acids naturally, so you need to include them in your diet. One of the best sources of omega-3 fatty acids is cold-water fish, such as salmon, mackerel, anchovies, sardines, and herring (think "SMASH"). If you don't consume enough fish, be sure to get your omega-3 fatty acids from other sources, such as canola oil, walnuts, and flaxseed.

In 2018, a systematic review and meta-analysis of studies regarding omega-3 and anxiety was published in the *Journal of the American Medical Association* (JAMA) Network Open and showed that omega-3 may help reduce clinical anxiety.

Vitamin C

A vitamin C deficiency can make you more stressed out.
TRUE

Vitamin C promotes healthy adrenal gland functions and helps you cope with stress.

Vitamin C enhances the immune system and promotes healing from infection, disease, and injury. It also helps the adrenal glands. Your adrenal glands (when properly functioning) help you cope with stress. Good food sources of vitamin C include:

- **Parsley**
- **Broccoli**
- **Bell peppers**
- **Strawberries**
- **Oranges**
- **Lemon juice**
- **Papayas**
- **Cauliflower**
- **Kale**
- **Mustard greens**
- **Brussels sprouts**

Vitamin B

A vitamin B deficiency can make you nervous and irritable.

TRUE

B vitamins influence the manufacture of specific neurotransmitters. For example, B_6 is needed for the manufacture of dopamine through the amino acids 1-phenylalanine and tyrosine. Thiamin (B_1) is needed for GABA synthesis. B vitamins are building blocks for some neurotransmitters and improve your ability to think clearly.

	FOODS RICH IN B VITAMINS	B-VITAMIN DEFICIENCIES
B_1	Oatmeal Peanuts Bran Wheat Vegetables Brewer's yeast	Decreased alertness Fatigue Emotional instability Decreased reaction time
B_2	Liver Cheese Fish Milk Eggs Brewer's yeast	Trembling Sluggishness Tension Depression Eye problems Stress
B_6	Wheat germ Cantaloupe Cabbage Beef Liver Whole grains	Nervousness Irritability Depression Muscle weakness Headaches Muscle tingling
B_{12}	Eggs Liver Milk Beef Cheese Kidneys	Mental sluggishness Confusion Psychosis Stammering Limb weakness
FOLIC ACID	Carrots Dark leafy vegetables Cantaloupe Whole wheat	Memory problems Irritability Mental sluggishness

Drink Enough Water

***There's no connection between drinking enough water and whether you feel anxious.*
FALSE**

If you don't replace that water, your body will set off warning signals in the form of anxiety-provoking sensations.

Your body is 80 percent water. So, besides feeding the brain the right foods, you also need to stay hydrated. In fact, you can survive without food longer than you can without water. Each day, you lose about 4 percent of your body weight in water through perspiring, urinating, defecating, and even breathing.

A small 2024 study in Spain with sixty-five female university students revealed that the women who were the most dehydrated were also the most anxious. It's possible that dehydration raises levels of the stress hormone cortisol. This may account for the fact that anxiety can become worse if you don't drink enough water.

MAKE IT A HABIT

Drink approximately six 10-ounce (295-ml) glasses of liquid (including milk and other noncaffeinated drinks) per day. If your mouth feels dry, drink.

Calcium, Magnesium, and Potassium

Eating foods high in calcium and magnesium help you remain calm.
TRUE

Calcium is a natural tranquilizer, and magnesium helps relieve anxiety, tension, nervousness, muscular spasms, and tics. Calcium and magnesium are also important to prevent tension. They tend to help relax a tense and overwrought nervous system. Good sources of calcium in foods are:

- **Dairy products, such as milk, yogurt, and cheese**
- **Oysters**
- **Canned salmon (especially the bones)**
- **Beans: Black beans, navy beans, cooked soybeans**
- **Mustard greens, bok choy, and cooked spinach**
- **Tofu and almonds**
- **Corn tortillas**
- **Calcium-fortified foods, such as fortified orange juice, cereals, waffles, and soymilk**

Potassium

Potassium balances the acid-to-alkaline ratio in your system, transmits electrical signals between cells and nerves, and even enhances your athletic performance. It works with sodium to regulate your body's water balance and is necessary for muscle function, energy storage, nerve stability, enzyme and hormone production, and your heart's health against hypertension and stroke. If you take blood pressure medication, you're vulnerable to potassium deficiency. Potassium helps oxygenate your brain for clear thinking. Stress, hypoglycemia, and acute anxiety or depression can result in potassium deficiency. Good food and herb sources of potassium are:

- **Fresh fruits, especially kiwis and bananas**
- **Potatoes**
- **Chile peppers**
- **Sea vegetables**
- **Lean poultry and fish**
- **Dairy foods**
- **Legumes, seeds and whole grain**
- **Vegetable broth**
- **Spices and herbs, such as parsley, coriander, cumin, basil, tarragon, ginger, dillweed, paprika, and turmeric**

Vitamin Supplements

Consider your diet, not vitamin supplements, the foundation of your health. There is no replacement for a healthy diet. However, sometimes additional vitamin supplements can be helpful, even if you do practice healthy eating habits. You can try a full-spectrum, once-a-day multivitamin along with a daily omega-3 capsule. Include a calcium supplement if you are lactose intolerant and take magnesium at the same time. Taking a calcium-magnesium supplement or drinking warm milk before bed improves sleep.

> **MAKE IT A HABIT**
>
> Add two to three foods with brain-nourishing nutrients to what you're currently eating. For example, add orange slices (vitamin C) and whole grains—think quinoa (protein) and brown rice (potassium)—to a salad. Make it a habit to regularly incorporate new nutrients into meals and snacks.

Master Food List

Go through the list of foods rich in vitamin B, C, calcium, magnesium, and potassium. Create a master list of brain-boosting foods that you'll enjoy eating. Each week choose at least two to three foods from this list and add them to your diet.

1 ....

2 ....

3 ....

4 ....

5 ....

6 ....

7 ....

8 ....

Five-Minute Habits

SKIP THE COFFEE BREAK.

Brew a cup of green tea instead. It's full of theanine, which boosts the production of neurotransmitters serotonin and dopamine.

PACK IN PROBIOTICS

Add serotonin-rich foods like pickles, sauerkraut, kefir, and plain yogurt to ease social anxiety.

SNACK ON DARK CHOCOLATE.

The antioxidants in dark chocolate quench free radicals that cause inflammation and can make anxiety worse.

DRINK A GLASS OF WATER.

If you're dehydrated, it will help calm your system.

Fine-Tune Your Body

03

How much do you know about how correct breathing practices, exercise, and sleep affect your anxiety level?

Take this quiz to find out >

YES

NO

(Y) (N) **Does anxiety make you breathe faster?**

(Y) (N) **Can you stop the fight-or-flight response by changing the way you breathe?**

(Y) (N) **Do breathing practices that focus on the stomach calm you down?**

(Y) (N) **Do stretching exercises reduce anxiety?**

(Y) (N) **Is aerobic exercise the only kind of movement that reduces anxiety?**

(Y) (N) **Is there anything I can do to get into the habit of exercising even if I don't want to?**

HABIT #1
Learn to Breathe to Relax

Does anxiety make you breathe faster?
YES

Most people take from nine to sixteen breaths per minute when they are at rest. By contrast, a person experiencing a panic attack can take as many as twenty-seven breaths per minute!

Rapid breathing can cause many of the symptoms associated with a panic attack, including numbness, tingling, dry mouth, and lightheadedness. When you breathe too fast, the muscles in your abdomen also tighten up and your chest cavity becomes constricted. When your breath is shallow, you also breathe too fast.

Catch Your Breath

Your cardiovascular system includes your respiratory system and your circulatory system. This is why rapid breathing causes your heart rate to speed up and increase anxiety. So, it makes sense that if you slow your breathing down, your heart rate will also slow, and you'll become more relaxed.

Breathing too fast is referred to as "hyperventilation" or "over-breathing." When you over-breathe, the balance of oxygen and carbon dioxide is disturbed. Because carbon dioxide helps maintain the critical acid base (pH) level in your blood, a higher pH level causes your nerve cells to become more excitable, and you can feel anxiety or associate the feelings with a panic attack.

Reduced levels of carbon dioxide lead to respiratory alkalosis, which makes your blood more alkaline and less acidic. Alkalosis constricts your blood vessels so that less blood flows through, which means less oxygen reaches the brain. So even though you're breathing quicky, less oxygen is available to your tissues.

Respiratory alkalosis also causes the blood vessels in your brain to constrict, which leads to dizziness, lightheadedness, feelings of unreality, and tingling in the extremities. If you're prone to panic attacks, you can over-respond to these physiological sensations and breathe even more quickly.

> **GRETA CATCHES HER BREATH**
>
> Greta called 911 because she thought she was having a heart attack. She told her doctor that it all started when she began to hyperventilate. "Soon, it felt like my heart was going to jump out of my chest. It seemed like it was ready to explode."
>
> Greta had had a series of similar episodes but none this severe. "It seemed like each attack was getting worse, and they all started with the breathing problem," she said. "I felt like I was going to suffocate and couldn't get enough air, no matter how hard I tried."
>
> Through therapy, Greta began to understand that she didn't have a heart problem and that she was suffering from the beginnings of a PD. Because her hyperventilation seemed to be the trigger for her panic symptoms, she started using the breathing exercises you'll learn in this chapter.

Counteract Fight-or-Flight by Breathing the Right Way

Can you stop the fight-or-flight response by changing the way you breathe?
YES

Breathing properly can help you gain a sense of self-confidence and can lead to a sense of being relaxed in general. While one of the symptoms of panic is shortness of breath, breathing slowly and deeply, especially with a longer exhalation, will help you relax. Start by noticing your breathing and when you feel anxious, stop and slow it down. To shift from the fight-or-flight response (activated by your sympathetic nervous system) to the relaxation response (activated by your parasympathetic nervous system), try these action steps:

1. *Hold your breath for 10 to 15 seconds. This temporarily prevents the dissipation of carbon dioxide.*

2. *Breathe in and out of a paper bag. You will re-inhale the carbon dioxide in the bag and restore the balance of oxygen and carbon dioxide in your bloodstream.*

3. *Exercise vigorously when you're anxious. This increases your metabolism and produces more energy. The inhaled oxygen is used up by the process of metabolism, and a larger quantity of carbon dioxide will be produced.*

4. *Practice deep abdominal breathing, which allows your lungs to fill to capacity. This slows your body down.*

Breathing Lessons

Do breathing practices that focus on the stomach calm you down?

NO

When learning to breathe to relax, focus on your diaphragm. When you breathe too fast, the muscles in your abdomen tighten up, and your chest cavity becomes constricted. You can reverse this by learning to breathe using a method that overemphasizes your diaphragm.

As you breathe abdominally, your belly rises when you inhale and drops when you exhale. This is because the diaphragm, the large dome-shaped muscle under your rib cage, expands and contracts. When you inhale, your diaphragm contracts and pulls down, as your abdominal muscles relax. This allows your lower lungs to expand, so that you can breathe deeply. When you exhale, your diaphragm moves back up, and your abdominal muscles contract.

Breathing Exercise 1

At any time during the day, whether you're at work, at home, or out and about and feel anxious, 4-7-8 Breathwork can calm you down. Developed by holistic expert Andrew Weil, M.D., the founder of the Andrew Weil Center for Integrative Medicine in Arizona, this breathing practice is easy to remember and practice. When you realize that you're feeling stressed, stop and inhale slowly through your nose to a count of 4, hold your breath for 7 counts and exhale slowly through your mouth to a count of 8. Repeat 4 times. Do it regularly and it will soon become a positive habit you can count on to feel better!

Breathing Exercise 2

1 *Lie on your back on a carpeted floor or bed. Put a pillow under your head and two pillows on your belly. This position allows you to watch the pillows rise as you use your diaphragm muscles to breathe. While inhaling, breathe through your nose. Now, take a deep breath and watch the pillows rise. While exhaling, watch the pillows go down.*

2 *While continuing to lie on your back, set aside the pillows and put your hand on your belly. Use the breathing techniques in Step 1 and notice your hand rising and falling with every inhalation and every exhalation.*

3 *Still lying on your back, place your arms at your side and follow the same breathing method. Notice your belly rise and fall with each inhalation and exhalation.*

4 *Now, sit on an easy chair or a sofa and watch your belly rise and fall with each inhalation and exhalation.*

5 *Sit up straight, in an upright chair, and repeat this breathing method. Make sure that your shoulders and chest are still.*

6 *Finally, stand up and repeat the exercise.*

Set aside 15 to 20 minutes to practice this exercise at least once a day. It's best if you practice this exercise in a quiet place where you won't be interrupted. Try to clear your mind of the day's concerns and consider it a break. If you don't have enough time, try the next exercise, which is an abbreviated version.

Breathing Exercise 3

The next exercise can be practiced sitting down and requires only a few minutes.

1 *Find a comfortable sitting position.*

2 *Put both feet on the floor with your arms at your sides.*

3 *Breathing in, fill your lungs with more air than you usually do.*

4 *Wait a moment before you exhale.*

5 *Slowly exhale more air than you think you can.*

6 *Inhale again and watch your belly rise.*

7 *Hold for a moment.*

8 *Exhale slowly.*

9 *Repeat this several times.*

Try any one of these abdominal breathing exercises the next time you feel anxious. Notice how some of your anxiety drifts away. Practice breathing on a regular basis, and do it often, so that it becomes your habitual way of breathing. Try to stop what you are doing every hour and slow down your breathing by breathing abdominally for at least thirty seconds.

HABIT #2
Stretch Away the Tension

Do stretching exercises reduce anxiety?
YES

Anxiety causes a buildup of tension and stretching relieves it. When you are anxious, and especially if you have GAD, which is characterized by constant worry, you may tighten your muscles. A lot of energy is wasted in maintaining muscle tension, which contributes to the fatigue GAD sufferers experience.

Suffering from anxiety can make you feel "all wound up." When chronic anxiety builds up in your muscles, the constant muscle tension overdevelops the connective tissue and makes the tendons thicken and shorten. Chronic anxiety also over activates the sympathetic nervous system, resulting in tension buildup in an already burdened system. The way to get rid of the buildup of tension is to stretch. If you have a sedentary lifestyle, you can also be vulnerable to tension buildup in your body. Because of your lack of movement, your muscles tighten up and atrophy. The tension that's "stored" in your body contributes to yet more anxiety because your body "feels tense."

To drive out tension and relax your muscles, you need to stretch. Your muscles are endowed with a rich blood supply, and stretching can promote better blood flow to your muscles. When you stretch your muscles, you force used, de-oxygenated blood back into the lungs for refueling. The re-oxygenated blood flows back out to your muscles, refreshing and invigorating them and helping you release tension.

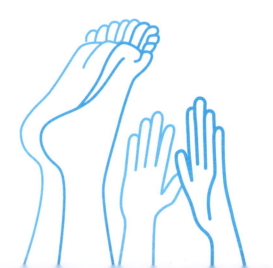

> **MAKE IT A HABIT**
>
> Take stretching breaks throughout the day to release tension and promote calm. Add variety and promote flexibility and balance by spending five to ten minutes doing yoga stretches like Downward Dog, Triangle, Cat/Cow, Bridge, and Child's Pose.

Practice Simple Stretches

Make it a habit to perform these stretches throughout the day. If you lead a sedentary life, perform at least one of these stretches once an hour. Or, in the middle of the day, try all of them, giving yourself at least a few minutes for each.

Chest Expander
While standing, widen your stance and stretch your arms up and to the side, making the figure of an **X,** while breathing in deeply. Exhale as you bring your arms back down to your sides.

Neck Roll
While sitting or standing, drop your chin to your chest, then slowly roll your head around 360 degrees. Then, roll it in the opposite direction.

Shoulder Shrug
While sitting or standing, raise your shoulders up to your ears. Then, roll your shoulders back. Imagine your shoulder blades touching. Next, drop your shoulders. Do this exercise slowly, several times.

Prayer/Hand Push
While standing or sitting, place your hands together in a prayer position close to your chest. With your elbows pointing downward, push both hands together.

HABIT #3
Move Your Body to Relax

Is aerobic exercise the only kind of movement that reduces anxiety?

NO

Walking, aerobic exercise, and even making small changes like taking the stairs can help reduce anxiety by promoting movement. Our bodies are designed to move. When it comes to anxiety, exercise plays a fundamental role in rebalancing your body and your brain and produces a natural tranquilizing effect. That's because physical exertion creates biochemical changes that can ease your anxiety. Here's why:

- *Exercise reduces muscle tension that tends to make you feel tense and anxious.*

- *Exercise rechannels bottled-up frustration that can contribute to anxiety.*

- *Exercise increases the metabolism of excess adrenaline and thyroxin (a hormone produced by your thyroid gland), which contributes to hypervigilance and tension, clearing them from your system.*

HOW TO OVERCOME EXERCISE AVOIDANCE

RATIONALIZATION	SOLUTION
I'm too anxious to exercise.	Exercise calms you down.
I don't have the time.	Break your exercise into 10-minute increments.
I don't belong to a gym.	Run, swim, or play tennis in your neighborhood.
I'm not athletic.	You can walk, cycle, swim, or climb stairs.
I'd rather do something fun that doesn't seem like exercise.	Join a dancing class, garden, or just dance to good music in your living room.
People will see me.	Invest in a treadmill or stationary bicycle and work out in the privacy of your home.
I'm too out of shape.	You'll get into shape by exercising. Start slowly.
I don't feel like it.	The biggest hurdle is getting started. When you keep at it, it becomes easier. Don't forget about the power of neuroplasticity.

More positive benefits of exercise:

- **Enhanced neurogenesis— new neurons emerge in the hippocampus**
- **Lower pH (decreased acidity) of your blood, which increases your energy level**
- **Improved circulation (including in your brain)**
- **Increased oxygenation of your blood and brain, which increases your alertness and ability to concentrate**

- **Improved digestion, which helps you make better use of the food you eat**
- **Improved elimination from your lungs, skin, and bowels**
- **Improved blood-sugar regulation**
- **Lower blood pressure (by lowering hypertension)**
- **Lower cholesterol levels**
- **Reduced insomnia**
- **Helps you lose weight**

Make Exercise a Habit

Walking and aerobic exercise, like running or cycling, all promote relaxation and a greater sense of well-being. Aerobic exercise can result in a "runner's high." This happens because this type of exercise results in the release of your body's endorphins, which are natural brain opiates. Not only do you experience a euphoric and calming feeling after you exercise, but your stress hormones are also reduced. Getting good exercise doesn't mean having to join an expensive health club, suit up in expensive workout gear, or run 5 miles (8 km) a day. Exercise can take any form.

Is there anything I can do to get into the habit of exercising even if I don't want to?
YES

You can overcome exercise avoidance by changing your perspective and routine. Exercise is good for you and good for your anxiety. But if you're anxious and feel pressured by a lack of time or energy, the thought of trying to squeeze it into an already crowded day just makes it worse. Whatever your reasons for avoiding exercise, the chart at left on the opposite page provides solutions.

Cultivate Calm

04

How much do you know about how to relax?

Take this quiz to check your "calm IQ" >

One of the best techniques for activating your parasympathetic nervous system (to counterbalance the *fight-or-flight* response) is:

(A) **The calm cure**

(B) **Stress reduction strategy**

(C) **The relaxation response**

(D) **A relaxation routine**

Using your imagination can help reduce anxiety. This is known as:

(A) **Affirmation**

(B) **Fact-finding**

(C) **Storytelling**

(D) **Visualization**

Self-hypnosis will:

(A) **Help you to relax**

(B) **Make you do things you don't want to do**

(C) **Prevent you from remembering anything**

(D) **Put you in a trance**

The benefits of meditation include:

(A) **Less stress**

(B) **Lower anxiety**

(C) **Clearer thinking**

(D) **All of the above**

HABIT #1
Practice the Relaxation Response

***One of the best techniques to activate
your parasympathetic nervous system is:***

The relaxation response

Feeling calm may seem like an experience enjoyed by people without anxiety, but not by you. How can they be so blessed? Are they just lucky, or are you cursed? Although it sounds impossible when you are suffering from anxiety, the good news is that you can *learn* to relax and be calm. You have that capacity built into your body.

As you learned in chapter 1, your autonomic nervous system has two branches: the sympathetic nervous system and the parasympathetic nervous system. The sympathetic nervous system activates your body; your parasympathetic nervous system calms it down. In this chapter, you'll relearn to tap into the talents of your parasympathetic nervous system.

Normally, the sympathetic and the parasympathetic nervous systems balance each other out. But when you suffer from anxiety, your sympathetic branch learns to dominate. Too much activation makes you anxious. You want to bring the two branches back into balance. To heal your anxiety, you need to tap into the skills of your parasympathetic nervous system so you can calm down.

Your parasympathetic nervous system has a counterbalance to the fight-or-flight response. Dubbed the "relaxation response" by Harvard professor Herbert Benson, it describes your body's parasympathetic nervous system in action. The relaxation response slows down your breathing and helps lower your heart rate and metabolism. Take a look at this chart and you'll see how the relaxation response and the fight-or-flight response balance each other out:

FIGHT-OR-FLIGHT RESPONSE

Sympathetic Nervous System

HEART RATE

BLOOD PRESSURE

METABOLISM

MUSCLE TENSION

BREATHING RATE

MENTAL AROUSAL

RELAXATION RESPONSE

Parasympathetic Nervous System

For thousands of years, people in societies across the globe have developed techniques to induce the relaxation response and activate the parasympathetic nervous system—without knowing of their existence. Practices such as prayer and meditation were devised to engender spirituality and a sense of inner peace.

You can activate the relaxation response in many ways. These include progressive relaxation, visualization, self-hypnosis, meditation, prayer, mindfulness meditation, and yoga. All of these methods promote relaxation and a sense of inner peace. Each of them utilizes the *Seven Principles of Relaxation.*

The Seven Principles of Relaxation

1. ***Breathing rhythmically*** • Deep, deliberate, and focused breathing allows you to slow your heartbeat and to center your attention on relaxation. You learned how to do abdominal breathing in the previous chapter.

2. ***Focused attention on the present moment*** • Much of anxiety is about nervous anticipation of the future. When you gently focus your attention on the here and now, you transform your experiences into rich and calm experiences.

   —

   Gentle focused attention activates your frontal lobes to exert their ability to inhibit the over reactivity of your amygdala.

   —

   Some practices include a "point focus." Focusing on your breathing or on a word, such as a mantra, while meditating can help you stay focused in the present.

> These seven principles can lower your anxiety by helping you "let go" of sympathetic nervous system arousal. Shifting your attention to accept and observe the present moment, while simultaneously breathing deeply, promotes relaxation. As a consequence, situations you once associated with anxiety can be experienced with a relaxed attitude. Each principle by itself can help defuse anxiety. When combined, they are particularly powerful in putting you at ease.

3   *A quiet environment* • A quiet environment gives you the opportunity to learn relaxation without distractions. Later, when you are unable to practice in a quiet environment, you can relate back to the way you felt in the quiet place to help you stay focused.

4   *An accepting and nonjudgmental attitude* • By shifting away from rigid expectations and to an accepting attitude, you'll appreciate reality as it is, rather than what you fear it could be.

—

In other words, by not "trying too hard" to relax, you take the pressure off yourself and can relax. Consequently, you'll free yourself to adjust to whatever happens. When you let yourself experience the here and now, instead of fearing the future, you'll be more relaxed and present.

5   *A relaxed posture* • This can include sitting in a relaxed posture or stretching, as you would when practicing yoga (see page 51).

6   *Observation* • By quietly observing each experience, you detach from the compulsion to immediately react to it. Observation allows you to detach from anxiety, by seeing your experiences "from a distance," as if you were not directly affected by them. When you observe your experiences in a nonjudgmental fashion, you simply note what is occurring at the time. Taking the vantage point of an observer, instead of a victim, allows you to detach from the anxiety.

7   *Labeling* • Labeling what you experience accesses your left frontal lobe and its positive emotions. This works if you remain in an accepting and non-judgmental attitude as a detached observer.

HABIT #2
Use Visualization to Achieve a Sense of Peace

Using your imagination can help reduce anxiety. This is known as:

Visualization

Your imagination is a powerful tool, and it can be used to heal your anxiety. You use your imagination every day for periodic daydreaming, so you might as well make it work *for* you, instead of against you. Don't forget that, in your daydreams, you're the star as well as the scriptwriter. This means that you can change the storyline to fit your goal of achieving relaxation. Just as you can imagine the worst, you can also imagine positive experiences. The therapeutic practice of imagery involves visualizing being in a safe, tranquil place that gives you a sense of peace. While you're there, use the *Seven Principles of Relaxation* to cultivate a state of peacefulness and calm.

Visualization Exercise
Find a quiet environment and get comfortable. Close your eyes and slow your breathing. Try this calming scenario to get you started:

1. *Imagine yourself walking on a secluded beach. The sun is warm on your skin, and there is a gentle sea breeze. You can smell the tang of the sea air.*

2. *Watch the waves roll in, one after the other, and notice the deep blue color of the sea out beyond the surf.*

3. *Stop and examine a tide pool; study the pebbly arms of a starfish and the waving fronds of the sea anemones.*

4. *Embrace all of the visual, auditory, and tactile sensations of the experience: the mist, the crash of the waves, the texture of the sand under your feet. Hear the sound of the surf as it ebbs and flows; make it match every inhalation and exhalation of your breath.*

5. *As you finish your visualization, concentrate on a flock of pelicans flying by in formation and taking your anxiety with it.*

Visualization can take you away from the anxiety of the day. If you fully absorb yourself in the calming imaginary scenes, you can soothe and refresh yourself. You will feel calm as well as revitalized.

TRY THESE VISUALIZATION SCENARIOS TO HELP YOU RELAX

A MOUNTAIN MEADOW

Imagine yourself in a mountain meadow in the fall. Smell the aroma of the pines and feel the coolness of the gentle mountain breeze. The leaves of the aspens clatter, and, as you gaze over to them, you notice that they are turning gold in the crisp autumn air. You see a mountain peak on the horizon with a rainbow overhead.

FLOATING ON A RIVER

Imagine yourself on a raft floating down a river. You don't need to paddle; instead you allow the easy current to take you down the river. You smell the lavender and sage that grows on the river's edge. You gaze at the lush, green trees on the bank of the river, the deer that graze below the canopy of a huge oak, and the birds in the sky.

WALKING IN A SNOWY FOREST

Imagine yourself walking into a forest. You look up and see the snow as it softly falls on the trees above and drifts to the forest floor. You feel the cold, crisp air on your face and smell the pine trees as the snow crunches underneath your boots. You hear small animals as they rustle through the leaves on the ground and see an eagle as it flies overhead to its nest.

✷

You can also create your own visualizations to help you relax. For more about visualization for calm and to achieve your goals check out Shakti Gawain's classic book *Creative Visualization: Use the Power of Your Imagination to Create What You Want in Your Life* (New World Library).

HABIT #3
Try Self-Hypnosis

Self-hypnosis will:

 *Help you to relax*

Self-hypnosis is an effective way to relax.

Hypnosis is a form of relaxation that uses breathing, imagery, focused attention, and increased receptivity to suggestion and direction, led by one trained in hypnotherapy. *Self*-hypnosis is a method of relaxation and absorption that you induce in yourself. It is easier to do than you might think. First, let's dispel a few myths about hypnosis.

MYTH	TRUTH
Hypnotic subjects are under the hypnotist's control.	You are actually in control. That's what self-hypnosis is about.
The same techniques are used for all people.	You can use whatever works for you.
A person in a hypnotic trance will not remember anything.	You will remember what you want to remember.
You can't get out of the trance without a ritual.	It's easy to shift your attention out of a trance.

Allow Your Body to Relax

When practicing self-hypnosis, it is particularly important to remind yourself that you can "step out of the way," so that your body can relax itself. If you allow your body to do what is natural, the process of self-hypnotic relaxation can unfold naturally.

Self-Hypnosis Exercise

A simple self-hypnotic experience uses focused breathing and counting down from 10 to 1. As the numbers decrease, imagine the parts of your body relaxing with each exhalation. Try the following steps, and use any of the phrases that fit for you.

10 ...... *I am allowing the tension to leave my body with every exhalation.*

9 ...... *I am feeling my body becoming heavy.*

8 ...... *Sounds, physical sensations, and worried thoughts are occurring around my external self, not deep within myself.*

7 ...... *I am descending deeper within myself, as if I am going down an escalator.*

6 ...... *I don't need to fight the relaxation. I can visualize myself drifting with the current down the river. I won't swim upstream, where anxiety lies.*

5 ...... *I am falling deep within myself like a feather that drifts to the ground without tension.*

4 ...... *I am deep within myself without worry.*

3 ...... *I am letting go of the old world of anxiety.*

2 ...... *Relaxation and I are one.*

1 ...... *I am at peace with myself in the present moment.*

Once you're completely relaxed, introduce calming posthypnotic suggestions such as:

- *I'm learning to put anxiety behind me.*
- *I no longer need to put myself on hyperalert.*
- *There's a calmer part of me that is expanding.*
- *Being calm and focused is my natural state.*

HABIT #4
Practice Meditation and Prayer

The benefits of meditation include:

 *All of the above*

Less stress • Lower anxiety • Clearer thinking

Meditation and prayer have a range of health benefits, including less stress, lower anxiety, and clearer thinking. Most religions have literature, including manuals, on meditation and prayer. Within Hinduism, Buddhism, Sufism, Judaism, and Christianity, meditation and prayer have a long tradition and have been practiced for thousands of years.

However, the psychological benefits were not well known until the twentieth century, when the positive effects of meditation and prayer were thoroughly researched and found to have a range of health benefits, including anxiety reduction. Experienced meditators can lower blood pressure and slow down their brain waves.

Meditation: A Mantra and the Breath

Most types of meditation involve allowing your mind to clear while focusing on your breathing. You clear your mind by concentrating on a few words, referred to as a "mantra," such as "Sat Nam." For example, you repeat the word "Sat" on the inhalations and the word "Nam" on the exhalations. By concentrating on the mantra and on your breath, your mind clears and your body relaxes.

Prayer: A Mantra and Faith

Prayer, when practiced not to achieve some reward, but to simply be closer to God, promotes a deep sense of inner peace. Many methods of praying involve repeating a phrase or entire verses, such as the Lord's Prayer. Like mantras, these phrases serve to direct your attention away from your worries and tension.

If you belong to a church, temple, or mosque, go often to engage in prayer for the purpose of relaxation and the peaceful feelings that you get from the experience, or you can practice prayer anywhere you choose. It can be helpful to use the Seven Relaxation Principles to remind yourself to breathe and relax in the present moment.

Make Mindfulness Meditation a Habit

Mindfulness meditation is a type of meditation derived from Buddhism, also referred to as "Vipassana" or "insight meditation," that can also help to reduce anxiety. This technique does not utilize a mantra or praying phrases. Instead, the focus is on breathing, observing, accepting, and employing a nonjudgmental attitude.

When you practice mindfulness, you observe and accept the thoughts, physical sensations, and emotions as they come in and out of your consciousness. You maintain a nonjudgmental attitude as you take a step back from your thoughts, physical sensations, and feelings, seeing them rise and fall back. When you adopt a mindfulness practice, you're incorporating many of the seven principles into your daily life.

Mindfulness has also been used in the treatment of chronic health problems, such as chronic pain. Instead of trying to block the pain, chronic pain sufferers learn to observe and accept the pain. This concept may seem strange, especially when considering pain. Why accept the pain? Doesn't it bring on more pain? The short answer is no. Mindfulness training can alter how your brain functions and lower your reactivity to pain because you're not trying to fight it. By observing and accepting the pain, you detach from its intensity.

Overall mindfulness practice has been shown to alleviate stress and cultivate positive feelings, such as the reduction of anxiety. One of the ways mindfulness lowers anxiety is through the connection between your prefrontal cortex and your amygdala. These connections can play a significant role in your resilience and the ability to maintain positive emotions in the face of adversity.

MINDFULNESS →

→ NOTICING ANXIETY →

→ LABELING EMOTIONAL STATE →

→ ACTIVATING
LEFT FRONTAL LOBE →

→ CALM

JOEL LEARNS MINDFULNESS MEDITATION

Joel complained about constant stress at work and had been suffering from GAD, with free-floating anxiety, tension, insomnia, and constant worries. To deal with his anxiety, Joel thought he would try meditation, but couldn't seem to get the hang of it. He said, "I sit down in that lotus position, and, at first, all I can think about is how my legs ache. Then my mind goes a mile a minute. The more I try to slow it down, the harder it gets."

Joel had a tendency toward trying to maintain control over every aspect of his life, which contributed to his GAD and his lack of success with meditation. The long-term goal was to help him let go of that compulsion.

Joel found that using the Seven Principles of Relaxation made mindfulness meditation easier. He tended to breathe shallowly but learned to breathe abdominally. Instead of sitting on the floor, he tried sitting in a comfortable chair.

While he meditated he simply observed his experience while meditating and shifted to an accepting and nonjudgmental attitude about any nuance or experience he encountered. For example, rather than say, "My neck hurts," he was to simply note that he was experiencing pain in his neck. When he tried this, he discovered that the pain in his neck faded away. When he felt some free-floating anxiety and worries nagged him like a pesky housefly, he didn't try to suppress them, but instead labeled them: "Oh, there's a few worries and some anxiety." When he labeled his observations, the intensity of his anxiety and the repetition of those worries drifted away.

Your Mindful Brain Reduces Anxiety

The areas of your brain that can defuse anxiety and tame your amygdala are the same areas that are activated when you practice mindfulness. One of these areas is your middle prefrontal cortex, which provides you with the skill of self-observation and has been described as the center of awareness. Long-term meditators are reported to have increased thicknesses of the middle prefrontal cortex as well as an enlarged right insula.

The right insula is an area of the cortex that monitors your body functions and, accordingly, how your body feels emotion. The middle prefrontal cortex and the right insula are the areas associated with empathy and self-awareness. The increased thickness of the middle prefrontal cortex is correlated with years of practice and reflects the neuroplasticity that occurred to strengthen this area so that it works more efficiently. When you narrate your experience, there is a shift in activation to the left prefrontal cortex.

Because your left prefrontal cortex is action-oriented, this activation allows you to put a positive spin on your experiences. When you activate your left hemisphere, there is a greater emphasis on approaching life and facing anxiety, rather than avoiding it, which occurs when you activate your withdrawal-oriented right hemisphere. Mindfulness involves the use of words, such as "I'm noticing an anxious thought," or "This is a little anxious," to label your emotional states. Labeling your emotions activates your frontal lobes and reins in the over reactivity of your amygdala.

Practicing Mindful Living

You only need a few moments to slow down your breathing and drop your shoulders. You can remind yourself throughout the day to take a few moments to relax by placing a blue dot on your wristwatch or computer. When you see the dot, stop for five seconds to collect yourself, breathe deeply, and meditate. Alternatively, you can identify certain objects as cues to relax. A doorknob or a desk drawer can serve as a reminder to take just a few moments and relax.

Relaxation Monitoring WORKSHEET

FORM OF RELAXATION	WEEKDAY	DURATION

MY FEELINGS BEFORE

MY FEELINGS AFTER

FORM OF RELAXATION	WEEKDAY	DURATION

MY FEELINGS BEFORE

MY FEELINGS AFTER

FORM OF RELAXATION	WEEKDAY	DURATION

MY FEELINGS BEFORE

MY FEELINGS AFTER

FORM OF RELAXATION	WEEKDAY	DURATION

MY FEELINGS BEFORE

MY FEELINGS AFTER

FORM OF RELAXATION	WEEKDAY	DURATION

MY FEELINGS BEFORE

MY FEELINGS AFTER

FORM OF RELAXATION	WEEKDAY	DURATION

MY FEELINGS BEFORE

MY FEELINGS AFTER

All these relaxation exercises require that you set aside some time for regular practice. It can be useful to structure it into your day. Use the worksheet at left to monitor your daily efforts and feelings before and after you practice. This will draw attention to how often you practice relaxation exercises and motivate you to practice more often.

MOVING FROM SELF-AWARENESS TO HIGHER CONSCIOUSNESS

Meditation and prayer help to shift your attention beyond personal concerns. When this happens, you move from a sense of self-identifying awareness to a higher consciousness. The effort to move beyond the personal to the transpersonal is consistent with a theology that conceptualizes your existence as only a small part of the totality of existence.

In meditation, when you sense the "wider reality"—that you are but a small part of a greater whole—you detach from the day-to-day attention to your worries.

Also utilizing the idea of a higher power, twelve-step programs are for everyone from recovering alcoholics to compulsive spenders. A popular slogan is: "Let go and let God." Many members find the process of turning over their problems to a higher power relieves their stress and anxiety.

This builds a sense of trust in themselves to handle what they can and a trust in something greater when it's time to let go. The *Serenity Prayer* encapsulates this approach:

God grant me the serenity to accept the things I cannot change, the courage to change the things I can, and the wisdom to know the difference.

If you have some issue that you're struggling with, it can be helpful to attend meetings, in-person or online, as an adjunct to the habits found here. Using the Serenity Prayer if you are experiencing anxiety can also help you to accept what is happening and move through it rather than fight the way you feel.

05
Change Your Thinking to Change the Way You Feel

Did you know that your thoughts can make you anxious? The good news is, there's plenty you can do to change your negative thinking, reduce your anxiety, and reclaim calm.

Take this quiz to find out >

TRUE

FALSE

(T) (F) *Basing your beliefs on how you feel reduces anxiety.*

(T) (F) *Activating your left frontal lobe, which is associated with positive feelings and action, can make you feel calmer and in control.*

(T) (F) *When you relabel your experiences so they're reality based, you feel less afraid.*

(T) (F) *Automatic thoughts or self-talk can be negative but have little effect on anxiety.*

(T) (F) *Practicing new, empowering assumptions will lower your anxiety.*

(T) (F) *Negative core beliefs can derail your recovery from anxiety.*

HABIT #1
Use Reality Testing to Reduce Anxiety

Basing your beliefs on how you feel reduces anxiety.
FALSE

Basing your beliefs on reality instead of your feelings reduces anxiety.

Your anxious feelings and thoughts have become bad habits that need to change. In fact, bad thinking habits can create and perpetuate anxious feelings. These are called "thinking errors." A thinking error can be as simple as the assumption that no one can be trusted. Or it can be more complex, such as believing that you are a psychologically damaged individual who will always suffer from anxiety because of a deeply wounded psyche.

The Problem with Being a Pessimist

Thinking errors lead to a heightened alert system and the fear that something bad is going to happen. You may think that if you expect the worst, that you won't be disappointed or think that if you obsess about a negative outcome that this will magically make things okay.

The problem is if you look at the glass half-empty, you feel more stress and on edge. You are always bracing yourself for the next challenge or problem. This can lead to constant worry and anxiety, trouble sleeping and more. It's like being a hamster on a wheel that never stops spinning.

Even worse, when you're in a heightened state of stress and anxiety, you also begin to see problems where none exist. This only adds to your burden and makes anxiety worse. You can begin to have panic attacks and feel out of control. Thinking errors, automatic thoughts, assumptions, core beliefs, negative self-talk, and pessimism can derail your day and your life. You expect the worst and set yourself up to experience the worst. But you can learn to shift away from a pessimistic outlook and construct a series of assumptions that help you react to events with greater adaptability. New thinking skills can allow you to adapt to changes in your life but also to consider those changes as opportunities.

Trapped by Thinking Errors = Anxiety

As you can see, when you become trapped by your thinking errors, anxiety can often result. So, it's essential to learn how to change the way you *think*, so that you can change the way you *feel*. Changing your thoughts is your starting point because it's easier than changing your feelings. It's also necessary. When you alter your thinking, your feelings will eventually change, too, and your anxiety will become more manageable.

Rather than expect the worst, you deal with what's actually happening in the present moment. You ground yourself in reality and calm yourself with the help of the exercises like abdominal breathing and mindfulness you've already learned about. This gets you off the hamster wheel, reduces anxiety, and makes you more resilient when stressful events do occur.

> **THE BOTTOM LINE?**
>
> How you think about new things affects how you're going to feel about them. So it's essential that you reframe the way you think to change the way you feel about the situations you encounter. Basically, you need to rewire your brain.

Adopting Habits to Rewire Your Brain for Calm

The more you repeat an action or think in a particular way, the more likely you are to turn these actions and thoughts into habits. These habits develop at the synaptic level through neuroplasticity, the process of making new connections between your neurons. When you learn habits that alert the frontal lobes of your brain to rein in your amygdala, it will help lower your anxiety level.

When you're plagued by anxiety, your amygdala—the part of your brain deep in your temporal lobes that is generally hyperactive in people with anxiety disorders—gets its way. Your amygdala hijacks your frontal lobes, which function to direct your attention, and override your ability to think clearly.

But you can learn to activate your left frontal lobe, so that you can regain control over your experiences. You can tame your amygdala by training your frontal lobes to recognize fact from fiction and "to decide" what not to be fearful of. Using reality testing—basing your beliefs on what is real and not on what you feel—you can control your fear center. In other words, you decide whether a threat really exists by looking at the facts of a particular situation, rather than on your feelings alone. For example, if you're feeling fear, and everything is actually okay, you can calm yourself by telling yourself that you're safe and all is well.

HABIT #2
Use Cognitive Restructuring to Reduce Anxiety

Activating your left frontal lobe, which is associated with positive feelings and action, can make you feel calmer and in control.
TRUE

The language skills of your left frontal lobe make the effectiveness of cognitive behavioral therapy (CBT) possible.

If you're like most people who suffer from anxiety, you underactivate your left frontal lobe, which is associated with positive feelings and action, and overactivate your right frontal lobe, which is associated with negative feelings and withdrawal. CBT addresses the cognitive distortions and thinking errors that underlie anxiety. Through cognitive restructuring—changing the way you think—you activate your left frontal lobe and confront the cognitive distortions and thinking errors. By cognitive restructuring, you confront the rigidity and boxed-in negativity head-on. You employ your underutilized left frontal lobe by:

Taking action

Reality testing

Verbal labeling

In other words, when you encounter a potential anxiety-provoking situation, you describe in realistic terms the challenge you face and then take action to meet the challenge. Because your left frontal lobe is capable of working with specific, bite-size details, it balances your right frontal lobe's tendency to be "big picture–oriented" and overwhelmed by anxiety.

HABIT #3
Verbally Relabel Experiences to Reduce Anxiety

When you relabel your experiences so they're reality based, you feel less afraid.
TRUE

When you relabel an experience, your left frontal lobe contributes its tendency toward positive feelings and its can-do attitude.

Also, the "approach tendency" works to counterbalance the withdrawal tendency of the right frontal lobe, especially during the critical exposure challenge, which you'll learn more about in the next chapter. Take a few minutes to determine whether you are mislabeling your experiences. Although the following list, on page 76, may seem rather obvious to you, you might be surprised by the number of statements you think are true. Do you have any of the mistaken beliefs on the following page? Circle "T" for true or "F" for false.

TIM PRACTICES VERBAL LABELING

Tim, a thirty-five-year-old librarian, had increasingly developed anxiety when in the presence of strangers. He hated it when his supervisor assigned him to the checkout desk, because he knew that he was expected to make small talk with patrons as they checked out books, and just the thought of it filled him with anxiety.

Tim began to practice verbal labeling techniques. He decided to identify and label a detail related to the book that a patron checked out. In this way, he could move away from feeling overwhelmed and shift to the detail-oriented and positive feelings of his left hemisphere.

As a patron came up to check out a book, Tim said, "Oh, *Cold Mountain*! That book has been one of our most popular ones for years. You'll enjoy it." "Thanks," said the patron. "I'll look forward to reading it even more now."

Tim managed to label a positive emotion by using the word "enjoy," even though it was about reading a book, and to make small talk at the same time. He proved to himself that he could pay attention to a positive detail outside of his feelings of anxiety and enjoy interactions with others.

Do You Mislabel Your Experiences?

T F *I have trouble with stress.*

T F *I should always be competent.*

T F *It is unwise to trust people.*

T F *Worrying about a problem lessens the severity.*

T F *Failing is horrible.*

T F *Sometimes it's hard to be alone.*

T F *I am embarrassed about my anxiety condition.*

T F *Life is often a struggle.*

T F *There is something fundamentally wrong with me.*

T F *When someone criticizes me, I am devastated.*

T F *My anxiety condition is hopeless.*

T F *I demand perfection from myself.*

T F *I can't control my emotions.*

T F *I'm beyond help.*

T F *My brain is defective*

T F *The damage is done and there's no going back.*

T F *Why set goals if I never achieve them?*

T F *My feelings tell me what to believe.*

Do You See Yourself Here?

T F *If I look into people's eyes, they'll know I'm nervous.*

T F *If my hair looks bad, it'll be a bad day.*

T F *A deep trauma occurred in my life.*

T F *Someone will find out that I'm incompetent.*

T F *Once people get to know me, they don't like me.*

T F *Life wears down my ability to cope.*

T F *I go from crisis to crisis.*

T F *My father made me feel nervous all the time.*

T F *One of these days, I'm going to lose it.*

T F *Someday, people will find out that I'm mentally ill.*

Many people tend to answer 'TRUE' to several of these statements. If you answered true to any of them, you are setting yourself up to feel more anxious and less in control of anxiety. This is because you box yourself in with expectations that give you little flexibility and room to be human. You need to restructure your beliefs, so that you have a fighting chance to manage your anxiety.

HABIT #4:
Change Your Automatic Thoughts to Reduce Anxiety

Automatic thoughts or self-talk can be negative but have little effect on anxiety.
FALSE

Automatic thoughts are bad habits that cloud fresh and positive experiences.

They can turn a potentially good experience into one fraught with anxiety. If you tell yourself that you are always stressed or full of anxiety before doing something new, that new experience will be tainted by that anxiety.

You are the narrator of your own life. The tone and perspective with which you describe each experience generates feelings associated with that narration. For example, if you find yourself constantly assuming, "This is hard," "I wonder whether I'm going to survive," or "It looks like this is going to turn out badly," you'll generate anxious feelings. It's time to restructure the way you think. Underlying this narration are the beliefs that frame your experience and give it meaning. Think of your beliefs as having many layers.

On the surface are your automatic thoughts. These are like short tapes that momentarily flash through your mind. Call these automatic thoughts a form of "self-talk" that you use as you navigate through the day. You produce a variety of these automatic thoughts, some consciously and some unconsciously.

For example, automatic thoughts that fuel anxiety go something like this: You walk into a room, see a few new people, and say to yourself, "Oh no, I don't like this. This is not good." Or "These people will soon find out that I am full of anxiety and will reject me."

Automatic Thoughts That Increase Anxiety and How to Deal with Them

Either/or thinking Simply put, either you feel anxious or you feel calm, and you believe there are no feelings in between. You constrain yourself into rigid thinking and have trouble thinking beyond black-or-white, either/or, and right-or-wrong possibilities. If you suffer from either/or thinking, develop the ability to see the shades of gray.

When you see new people, instead of telling yourself that the situation is terrible, learn to get comfortable with these unfamiliar people. For example, Josh, a museum tour guide, learned that it was natural to feel a little anxiety when meeting the new people on his tours. The anxiety helped him stay on his toes and explain things when museum visitors seemed confused.

If Josh thought in an either/or way, his minor anxiety would become overwhelming, and he would lose his capacity to be alert. Instead, he acknowledged a little anxiety as normal, which helped him defuse the potential to be overwhelmed with the assumption that a little anxiety is too much anxiety.

Overestimating or exaggerating risk If you walk outside and see a few clouds, you automatically assume a major storm is on the way and that your house will be flooded. When you regularly expect disaster, you increase your anxiety. Exaggerating risk is a less extreme, but more common, version of catastrophizing (which you'll read about later in this chapter). For example, the presence of a new person may stir thoughts that he will threaten your safety. On the other hand, the new person is someone you don't yet know anything about, so why jump to conclusions?

Barbara faced a challenge when she said goodbye to her old friends next door and new people moved into the house. Not only did she feel the loss of good friends, but she was also now faced with getting to know her neighbors, which made her anxious, because she didn't think she had the social skills to get to know them. It had taken her a few years to get to know her old neighbors, and the friendship developed largely because of their efforts. Barbara eventually decided that the loss of her friends didn't have to be a catastrophe. It became an opportunity to meet new people.

Emotional reasoning You say to yourself, "I have a gut feeling that something is going to go wrong." The problems with this gut feeling are that it is a false alarm and that you feel it too often. You might regard a particular emotion as evidence of the truth, instead of looking at the facts. An example is thinking, "I feel nervous, so it must mean something bad is going to happen." To challenge this faulty reasoning, you need to look at the facts and tell yourself, "I know I feel anxious, but there is no evidence that there is anything to feel anxious about." Reality testing simply means that you base your beliefs on what you know to be true—on what you have hard evidence for rather than your feelings, which may often be fearful.

Overgeneralizing You hear on the morning radio traffic report that there is a backup on a particular highway, so you assume that all the roads are jammed. This thinking error occurs when you use small pieces of information or details to paint a broad, entirely negative picture. This is worse than thinking that the glass is half-empty—it's believing that the glass has nothing in it at all. Kathleen fell into this thinking trap. Always called a "drama queen" by some of her friends at college, she had a tendency to label a class a "grade killer" if the professor lectured without using a PowerPoint program. She'd work herself up into such an anxiety state that her grades suffered because she found it hard to concentrate. Meanwhile, her classmates adapted to the unique format of the professor.

Track Your Automatic Thoughts and Correct Them

You need to replace bad thinking habits with good thinking habits by generating new automatic thoughts to refute and contradict the old negative automatic thoughts. Let's say you feel a panic attack coming on. If you don't change your thinking—and the negative self-talk that goes with those thinking errors—your old automatic thoughts will turn everything into a catastrophic experience.

In the left column of the chart below, you'll find negative automatic thoughts. In the right column are alternatives you can use to refute those automatic thoughts. Do any of these negative thoughts sound familiar? Notice how the corrective automatic thoughts give you flexibility to be human and grow. The corrective automatic thoughts bring in reality and hope.

AUTOMATIC THOUGHTS

OLD AUTOMATIC THOUGHTS	CORRECTIVE AUTOMATIC THOUGHTS
I'm stressed out because I have too much to do.	I can get things done, even if I'm a little anxious.
Oh my God! Here it goes again.	This happened before and I survived it.
Something terrible will happen.	But nothing terrible ever does happen.
I need to get out of here.	I can stay right where I am.
This will always happen.	Not if I change things.
I need help.	I can and will help myself.
They'll discover that I'm nervous.	If they do, it's no big deal.
He sees right through me.	I have nothing to hide.
They're all relaxed.	Good. And I can be, too!
There are too many people here.	There are more people to get to know!

Adopt Automatic Thoughts That Make You Feel Better

You can develop automatic thoughts that will make you feel better rather than trigger anxiety. These thoughts can help you turn a stressful experience into a positive one:

- *This problem or challenge is an opportunity.*
- *I can do this.*
- *I can cope with how things turn out.*
- *Things will look up soon.*
- *I'll do the best that I can.*
- *This will be a valuable learning experience.*
- *I can appreciate the shades of gray.*
- *I'll use my mind to judge the situation, not my feelings.*
- *I can learn to be more accepting of anxiety.*
- *Here's an opportunity to meet new people.*
- *I can adapt to this situation, even if I don't like it.*
- *This is interesting, even if it is a bit bizarre.*
- *I can enjoy myself, even when I'm anxious.*
- *A little anxiety is good—it keeps me alert.*
- *I'll focus on the positive, despite the negative people.*

You probably have a variety of your own automatic thoughts. Use the worksheet on the opposite page to write down the negative automatic thoughts that fuel your anxiety, then refute them with corrective automatic thoughts. Make sure the corrective automatic thoughts include flexibility and promote adaptability. Copy this list and carry it with you so that you can refer to it often. Practice these often, so that they become new habits.

> **MAKE IT A HABIT**
>
> Take a moment to construct a variety of new automatic thoughts. Practice them on a regular basis, so that your brain can rewire and make them new habits. Practice self-talk using them so that they become new automatic thoughts. Approach this exercise by developing automatic thoughts that are positive, hopeful, optimistic, and adaptive.

New Automatic Thoughts WORKSHEET

OLD AUTOMATIC THOUGHTS	CORRECTIVE AUTOMATIC THOUGHTS
I'm stressed out because I have too much to do.	I can get things done, even if I'm a little anxious.

HABIT #5
Adopt Anxiety-Reducing Assumptions

Practicing new empowering assumptions lowers anxiety.
TRUE

Just as you did with automatic thoughts, you can develop many anxiety-reducing assumptions that will serve you better than those that trigger anxiety. Here are several that can help you turn a stressful experience into a positive one:

- **I'm learning new coping skills**
- **I'll do the best I can, and that will be good enough**
- **I can appreciate the full range of possibilities**
- **I'm becoming more confident**
- **I'm just as worthy as the next person**
- **I don't need to control every detail in my life**

Take a moment to construct your own unique assumptions. Make sure that your new assumptions give you flexibility and do not contain such words as "should," "must," "never," "always," and "everyone." You'll be coming back to this list often to help you stay focused on what you need to practice.

Keep this list with you, so you can refer to it often. You can add to and fine-tune it to make it apply to the changing circumstances in your life. Practice these regularly, so that your brain can rewire and develop new habits. By rewiring your brain through repetition, you'll create a new set of healthy assumptions.

TIA'S NEW ASSUMPTIONS

After struggling with feelings of anxiety and periodic panic attacks for ten years, Tia decided she finally needed help. So, she attended an anxiety class. It became evident that she limited herself with many negative assumptions and was convinced that she had bad genes.

She assumed that she needed to avoid stress at all costs. But, because she avoided potentially stressful events, what she soon assumed to be too stressful were events and situations that she had managed to cope with in the past.

During the anxiety class, her peers shared their negative assumptions, such as "I'm beyond help now. My problems are unique. What helps others won't help me." She identified with each of them. However, when they told her that they soon got over those negative assumptions and replaced them

with positive assumptions, Tia said, "I think I'm too far gone." Almost in a chorus, her fellow class members said, "That's what we thought, too." With the encouragement of her peers, Tia began to shift from negative assumptions to positive ones.

Specifically, she shifted from "I'm beyond help now" to "I'm seeking help." And "My problems are unique" became "I can see that others have had similar problems." And finally, "What helps others won't help me" became "I don't know whether they won't help unless I try." Try she did.

Over the next few weeks, she managed to untie herself from the constraints of her negative assumptions and open herself up to the potential for change.

HABIT #6
Restructure Your Negative (and Stressful) Core Beliefs

Negative core beliefs can detail your recovery from anxiety.
TRUE

Negative core beliefs keep you from believing that you can find relief from anxiety. They set you up to fail because you leave yourself no hope.

Core beliefs are broad generalizations about yourself and how the world works. When the beliefs are associated with anxiety, they paint you into a corner psychologically, so that whatever you do, you're faced with an insurmountable challenge—one that will always fail.

Negative core beliefs can include the assumption that you are a deeply damaged person or that you don't have what it takes to make use of help. By changing your assumptions, as you did in the worksheet, you can chip away at your anxiety-producing core beliefs.

Another way of dealing with your core beliefs is to confront them directly. Many of your core beliefs developed as you were growing up. Perhaps your parents taught you that the world was a dangerous place and that you always needed to be on your guard. Or maybe you were led to believe that you were inadequate and incapable of succeeding.

Other core beliefs can form as you either succeed or fail at projects and major challenges during your life. If you succeeded, you developed feelings of adequacy; if you failed, you might have developed feelings of inadequacy. Perhaps you had some unfortunate social experiences, such as being rejected or ridiculed, or were told you were inadequate. Core beliefs include:

- **The world is a dangerous place: Life is a struggle, and things always go wrong**
- **I'm defective / I'm inadequate**
- **My mother damaged me deeply**
- **I was traumatized by childhood abuse and neglect and can't recover**
- **I took too many drugs in my youth, and there's nothing left of my brain**

- **God is making me pay for my sins**
- **I had a breakdown and there's no pulling it all back together**
- **I will always be dysfunctional because I know no other way of being**
- **I'm jinxed to have bad luck and anxiety around people.**
- **People can't be trusted**

DO YOU SEE YOURSELF HERE?

If you do, it's likely that one or more these core beliefs can rachet up your anxiety:

THE PERFECTIONIST

If you think of yourself as a perfectionist, you set yourself up to be disappointed in yourself, because nothing turns out perfectly. Because things don't work out perfectly, you might think that you are inadequate or have failed. By being locked into expecting perfection, you drive yourself into anxiety. Allow yourself to be human, which by definition is to be imperfect.

THE PESSIMIST

By thinking of yourself as a pessimist, you create a self-fulfilling prophesy. You'll expect the worst and feel the anxious emotions associated with the worst. You'll also do little to promote the best because you don't expect that it's possible. You might say to yourself, "Why try? Things always turn out badly."

THE VICTIM

If you feel you are a victim, you will feel victimized by whatever happens, no matter how negative or positive the experience. Ironically, your victim role can make you easy prey to those who are in the habit of taking advantage of people like you. This is because bullies tend to pick on people who are easy to manipulate. You can also develop an identity of being a martyr or a codependent. In this case, you feel that it is your job to take care of those who take advantage of you.

THE CRITIC

Being critical of events or situations is easy in the short term, because it's not hard to find imperfections. But in the long run, it's hard on you because you'll find fault with everything, including yourself. And because nothing in life is without faults, you end up feeling bad. Constant criticism increases your tension and anxiety, because finding fault puts you and those around you on edge.

Get Rid of Thinking Traps by Refuting Old Core Beliefs

These and other core beliefs are thinking traps that you can refute by developing counter-beliefs. Consider the following examples of core beliefs. See how you can refute them with beliefs in the column on the right.

CORE BELIEFS

OLD CORE BELIEF	REFUTED CORE BELIEF
I should be able to do things perfectly.	**I can allow myself to be human.**
I expect the worst—for good reason.	**There's no reason to expect the worst.**
Bad things happen to me.	**Both good and bad things happen to me.**
There is always something wrong.	**There's often a silver lining.**
My future was damaged early in life.	**I can write my own future.**
Anxiety is who I am.	**Anxiety is a bad habit that I'll break.**
Anxiety is a family tradition.	**It is a tradition that I will leave.**
I'm a worrier.	**I will learn to worry less.**
I'm different from others.	**Everyone is different.**
There are too many people here.	**There are more people to get to know!**

Refute Your Stressful Core Beliefs WORKSHEET

Core belief thinking traps can lead to anxiety. They all share a common tendency to "lock in" expectations of how things "ought to be." Use the worksheet to identify the core beliefs that fuel your anxiety. Refute these core beliefs in the column on the right. Your job is to restructure your core beliefs, so that you can defuse your anxiety.

OLD AUTOMATIC THOUGHTS	CORRECTIVE AUTOMATIC THOUGHTS

Develop Core Beliefs That Serve You

It is critical that you develop more effective core beliefs that will serve you much better than those that trigger anxiety. The new core beliefs will form the foundation for your assumptions and automatic thoughts. Once you develop new core beliefs, you'll need to recite them to yourself often so that they become part of you. Here are some that can help you turn a stressful experience into a fresh and positive one:

- **I'm a capable person**
- **I'm a worthwhile and worthy person**
- **I'm flexible and adaptable**
- **I don't allow people or situations to victimize me**
- **I can find silver linings in situations**
- **I mean well and try hard, and that is enough**
- **I can turn an awkward social situation into something enjoyable**
- **When people get to know me, they think I'm funny**
- **I'm an optimist, even around pessimistic people**
- **I hunger for personal growth and challenge**

Cultivate and Construct New Core Beliefs

Now, take a few moments to identify the core beliefs that you would like to cultivate. In other words, instead of simply refuting core beliefs, construct *new* ones that are fresh and have vitality, strength, adaptability, perseverance, resilience, and optimism. For example:

- *If you think of yourself as a spiritual and compassionate person, your new core belief could be: "I'm kind, generous and loving. The Universe supports me."*

- *Or maybe you'd like to cultivate a sense of adventure. Your new core belief could be: "I can travel the world by myself and meet new people along the way."*

- *Perhaps your new core belief can help you define yourself as a person who is capable, adaptive, and resilient: "I bounce back from adversity. I'm like a duck—water rolls off my back."*

New Core Beliefs WORKSHEET

MAKE IT A HABIT

Refer to your core beliefs worksheet often, just as you did with the automatic thoughts and assumptions worksheets. Reflect on how these new core beliefs are fundamental to your self-esteem and to the way you see yourself.

DIANE CHANGES HER THINKING

Diane, a computer engineer, was increasingly worried about the longevity of her job. Always worried that she would be laid off, she developed a heightened alert system that a layoff might soon happen. Trapped by her own thinking errors, she developed anxiety.

Diane prided herself on being a pessimist. She told friends that if she expected the worst, she would never be disappointed.

When situations did get tough, Diane was the one who felt the most stress. Her peers seemed to take it all in stride, yet she felt on edge all the time. Over time, as she braced herself for the next challenge or problem, she began to have trouble sleeping and worried constantly.

When the company was bought out, her peers continued to do fine in the face of what Diane thought was great stress. She would walk into a staff meeting, look around, and see that everyone seemed relaxed. She, in contrast, grew to dread staff meetings, often saying on the way in, "Well, let's see what management throws at us now. They want us to fail."

Soon Diane began to have panic attacks during the meetings. She would excuse herself and rush to the bathroom. The panic attacks convinced her that something was seriously wrong with her. One day, her panic attack was so acute that she went to the emergency room, convinced that her shortness of breath was evidence of a heart attack.

After his examination, the emergency room physician told her that her heart was fine and that, in fact, she had had a panic attack. After that, Diane began working with the techniques you learned in the preceding chapters, such as abdominal breathing and mindfulness. It quickly became clear that she suffered from thinking errors and negative self-talk.

She explored her automatic thoughts, assumptions, and core beliefs, and discovered that she harbored a deep-seated pessimism; she expected the worst and actually set herself up to experience the worst. For example, if she and her fellow employees received a bonus check, she assumed that management would soon demand that they work overtime without pay to recover the money from the bonus check.

It became evident that she constructed her beliefs with such rigidity and negativity that they offered her no option but to feel anxious in response to new experiences, including new assignments at work. Although she wanted to be positively surprised by these new experiences, she painted herself into a psychological corner by viewing new situations in a narrow and negative context, so that she wouldn't be disappointed.

It became evident that she constructed her beliefs with such rigidity and negativity that her only option was to feel anxious in response to new experiences, including new tasks at work. Gradually, Diane learned to shift away from her pessimistic outlook and construct a series of assumptions that helped her react to events with greater adaptability. Her new thinking skills allowed her to adapt to changes at work and convert them to healthy challenges instead. It was only after she changed her thinking habits that she was able to prevent panic attacks and deal with stress much more effectively.

Facing Your Fears

06

Directly confronting what you fear can be hard to do, especially if you have an anxiety disorder. Do you know how to face and overcome your fear?

Take this quiz to find out >

YES

NO

(Y) (N) **Before you address your avoidance behaviors, you need to identify them.**

(Y) (N) **If you face your fears, you only need to do it once to retrain your brain.**

(Y) (N) **You only need to imagine yourself dealing with a situation that creates fear and you'll be able to overcome it.**

(Y) (N) **Gradually exposing yourself to the things you fear will reduce your anxiety over time.**

Avoiding What You Fear Makes Anxiety Worse

This fact is difficult to grasp, because when you avoid what you fear over the short term, your fear temporarily decreases. Over the long term, however, avoidance allows that anxiety to flourish. Say, for example, that you are anxious about going to a party because you fear talking to strangers. When you avoid the party, your anxiety lessens. But if you avoid the next party invitation and then the next and the next, you now have a problem, because your avoidance has made your anxiety about talking to strangers worse than it was to begin with.

PAMELA'S AVOIDANCE BEHAVIORS

Pamela had been feeling ill at ease since she moved to a new condo complex. She didn't know the neighbors and felt awkward about starting at square one, introducing herself and getting to know them. She thought that because the other condo owners all knew one another, they were on firmer ground when socializing at parties at the complex. She would be under a spotlight, singled out as the "new person."

So, when Pamela was invited to the parties, she found convenient excuses to bow out. Yet, each time she turned down an invitation, she worried that the other owners would think of her as antisocial. Soon, her anxiety increased to the point where she avoided engaging with them at all. When she saw one of her neighbors in the parking lot, she pretended she didn't see them or that she had forgotten something in her car and ducked her head back in to hide.

Pamela's discomfort over socializing with others in the complex had become such a problem that she worried constantly about what might happen if she found herself in a situation where she had no choice but to say something, such as when she and a neighbor were standing next to one another.

She was losing sleep and felt tense much of the time. She also suffered from free-floating anxiety. Her avoidance had actually become the problem. When this was brought to her attention, she responded by saying, "Why not stay away from what is making me anxious? When I feel more at ease, I'll start talking to all of them." This is like being in quicksand, and, until she got out, she would just sink deeper. Pamela had to learn to avoid her avoidance and face her fears.

Challenging the Paradox: Replacing Avoidance with Exposure

In this chapter, you'll learn to work against avoidance, even though avoidance seems to make you feel better. This is called "challenging the paradox." It involves doing away with avoidance and replacing it with *exposure*—facing what makes you feel anxious.

By exposing yourself to anxiety-provoking situations, you become habituated to them, and your anxiety will actually diminish over the long term. Before discussing the ways to neutralize anxiety by exposure, it will be helpful to determine the degree to which you are engaging in avoidant behaviors. Answer the following questions by circling "Y" for yes or "N" for no.

Avoidance Questionnaire WORKSHEET

Do you...

Y N **Try to avoid situations that make you anxious?**

Y N **Continually monitor your anxiety level?**

Y N **Find increasingly "effective" ways to avoid anxiety?**

Y N **Search situations for things that may cause anxiety?**

Y N **Find that the range of your activities has shrunk?**

Y N **Think that any anxiety is bad anxiety?**

Y N **Avoid challenges that might be stressful?**

Y N **Procrastinate often?**

Y N **Avoid social situations that are challenging?**

Y N **Abruptly leave a situation if it stirs up anxiety?**

Y N **Find ways to distract yourself from anxiety?**

Y N **Isolate yourself from people you find intimidating?**

Y N **Avoid any form of stress more than you did a year ago?**

Y N **Carry around an anti-anxiety pill, just in case?**

Y N **Sit at the back of a room so you can easily escape?**

Y N **Offer your opinion only if forced?**

Y N **Consider those who don't share your opinions scary?**

Y N **Go to the same restaurant because it's familiar?**

Y N **Want to go back to when the world was simpler?**

If you answered 'YES' to any of the above questions, you are embracing avoidance over exposure. The greater the number of yes responses you circled, the greater your degree of avoidance and the greater the probability that you are promoting anxiety.

Forms of Avoidance

Several types of avoidant behaviors contribute to anxiety. They include escape, avoidance, procrastination, and safety behaviors. Do you see yourself here?

Escape behaviors are things you do in the heat of the moment when you are in an anxiety-provoking situation. You essentially escape the situation to flee from anxiety. Say, for example, that you are in a room with a crowd of people and you begin to feel anxious. Abruptly fleeing the room is an escape behavior.

Avoidance behaviors are things you do to stay away from anxiety-provoking experiences. Perhaps a friend invites you to meet him at the home of one of his colleagues. Because you don't know your friend's colleague, you decide that going to his home would provoke intolerable anxiety, so you don't go. That's an avoidance behavior.

Procrastination means that you put off things because it's "easier" on your stress level. For example, you put off going to the colleague's home, waiting until the very last moment to finally go. That's procrastination.

Safety behaviors are things that you do or carry with you to distract you or give you a sense of safety. Say you go to the colleague's home to meet your friend and begin to feel anxious. To prevent yourself from tumbling into a panic attack, you begin to fiddle with your watchband to draw your focus away from the others. That's a safety behavior.

All of these methods of dealing with anxiety are ways of staying away from anxiety. They are all forms of avoidance, and they keep you from habituating to the situation and learning to overcome the anxiety.

Short-Term Relief, Long-Term Problems

Because avoidant behaviors result in a temporary reduction of fear, they serve as powerful short-term reinforcements. They are, therefore, difficult to resist. Soon your avoidance can become increasingly elaborate. If taken to the extreme, you can become agoraphobic, afraid to leave your home. Once you begin avoiding, it's difficult to stop. Why is it so easy to use avoidance?

- *It reduces fear in the short term.*

- *There is a superficial logic to avoidance: "Why wouldn't I avoid something that makes me anxious?"*

- *You receive some secondary gain from it, such as extra care, because people around you feel sympathy.*

When Avoidant Behaviors Become Bad Habits

Avoiding situations that cause anxiety starts a destructive spiral. The more you engage in avoidant behaviors, the harder it is to resist repeating them in the future, because they become habits. Even distraction is a mild form of avoidance. When you distract yourself from anxiety-provoking situations, you are not getting the full positive (yes, positive!) effect of the exposure. Here's how it works:

Learning requires attention, and attention is directed by your frontal lobes. If you focus your attention somewhere other than on the situation in front of you, your frontal lobes do not direct your full resources to habituating yourself to it and making it routine.

Shifting your attention away from a situation prevents you from learning how to habituate to the situation. An obsession with being in control can also lead to avoidance. By trying to control every experience to minimize anxiety, you put yourself into a mode of always trying to anticipate the future, so that you can steer yourself away from the *possibility* of anxiety. Here's where your avoidant behaviors can get rather elaborate.

When you anticipate what *might* happen, you brace yourself for anxiety that you might not experience. Anxiety often results from anticipating the worst-case scenario. When you avoid situations, you put yourself at a realistic disadvantage, because you never get to prove to yourself that the worst rarely happens. You put yourself on hyperalert for detecting anxiety-provoking experiences, then perceive even minor events as dangerous.

Complete Control Is Impossible; Try Emotional Flexibility Instead

Trying to control your emotions is a tricky business. Complete control is impossible. Not allowing yourself to experience a moderate degree of emotional flexibility sets you up to constantly brace for an emotion outside your tolerance level. This is especially true if you are rigid about anticipating the future.

If you try to minimize "stress" at any level, you'll tend to avoid anything requiring the slightest degree of adjustment. Ironically, everything you encounter requires some degree of adjustment. The result is constant anxiety, because you can't control your emotions.

HABIT #1
Identify Your Escape, Avoidance, Procrastination, and Safety Behaviors

Before you address your avoidance behaviors, you need to identify them.
YES

The first step in developing an exposure plan is to recognize your escape, avoidance, procrastination, and safety behaviors.

To help you identify your behaviors, use the worksheets on pages 97-100. Add to the lists as you discover new behaviors that are working against you. You'll use these worksheets for your exposure exercises later in this chapter.

Escape Behaviors

Escaping situations can make you feel bad about yourself, which just uses up emotional energy you can use to overcome your fears. What's most important is realizing that when you escape, you don't give yourself a chance to adjust to what triggered your anxiety and to minimize that fear. Use this worksheet to identify your fears and the escape behaviors associated with them, which is critical for defusing your anxiety. Use the example given as a prompt.

> **MAKE IT A HABIT**
>
> Come back to this list over time and write down the new ways that you procrastinate. This task alone can help you minimize procrastination because you're becoming more aware of doing it. It can also motivate you to do it less often, because you must write it down and be accountable to yourself.

Escape Behavior Identifier WORKSHEET

WHAT I FEAR Meeting new people

HOW I ESCAPE Leave a room if a stranger enters

WHAT I FEAR

HOW I ESCAPE

WHAT I FEAR

HOW I ESCAPE

WHAT I FEAR

HOW I ESCAPE

WHAT I FEAR

HOW I ESCAPE

WHAT I FEAR

HOW I ESCAPE

WHAT I FEAR

HOW I ESCAPE

WHAT I FEAR

HOW I ESCAPE

WHAT I FEAR

HOW I ESCAPE

Avoidance Behaviors

Now, let's identify your avoidance behaviors. Use the following worksheet to identify your fears and the avoidance behaviors associated with those fears. Remember that these are things you do to avoid anxiety-provoking situations before you even encounter them. This list of your avoidant behaviors will also be useful later when you move on to the exposure exercises. Although you might find it hard to believe now, you'll turn back to this list later for a perspective on how far you've come.

Avoidance Behavior Identifier WORKSHEET

WHAT I FEAR *Meeting new people*

HOW I AVOID IT *Avoid social events of any kind*

WHAT I FEAR

HOW I AVOID IT

WHAT I FEAR

HOW I AVOID IT

WHAT I FEAR

HOW I AVOID IT

WHAT I FEAR

HOW I AVOID IT

WHAT I FEAR

HOW I AVOID IT

Procrastination

Procrastination is a tricky type of avoidance. You tell yourself that you aren't actually going to escape or avoid what you fear altogether. You tell yourself instead that you'll get to it later. But when? Usually it's at the last minute. Sometimes you wait so long that you must rush, which makes your performance subpar. When you procrastinate and perform poorly, you add to your stress and anxiety. Procrastination also heightens your anticipatory anxiety because you put off what you are dreading and hold back on taking action. It's like pressing the gas pedal and the brakes at the same time.

Procrastination Identifier WORKSHEET

WHAT I FEAR — Talking to strangers

HOW I PROCRASTINATE — Ignore them until they talk to me

WHAT THE RESULT IS — My fear increases

WHAT I FEAR

HOW I PROCRASTINATE

WHAT THE RESULT IS

WHAT I FEAR

HOW I PROCRASTINATE

WHAT THE RESULT IS

WHAT I FEAR

HOW I PROCRASTINATE

WHAT THE RESULT IS

WHAT I FEAR

HOW I PROCRASTINATE

WHAT THE RESULT IS

Safety Behaviors

Remember that safety behaviors are ways that you distract yourself when you are anxious. Initially, they can be useful to help you stay in a situation that makes you anxious. But the more you continue to use them, the more they become a method of avoiding your anxiety.

Identify your safety behaviors in the worksheet below. By identifying your safety behaviors, you can address these last vestiges of avoidance, which paradoxically increase your anxiety.

Safety Behavior Identifier WORKSHEET

WHAT I FEAR
Talking to strangers in a store

SAFETY BEHAVIOR
Pretend to talk on my phone

WHAT I FEAR

SAFETY BEHAVIOR

WHAT I FEAR

SAFETY BEHAVIOR

WHAT I FEAR

SAFETY BEHAVIOR

WHAT I FEAR

SAFETY BEHAVIOR

Some forms of distraction are useful at the beginning of an exposure exercise. For example, when you are attempting to conquer your fear of public speaking, it can be useful to focus on one person in the audience as a distraction. Later, you expand your attention to include the wider audience. But if safety behaviors continue, they outlive their usefulness. They make it difficult for you to habituate to anxiety-provoking situations. In addition to distracting you from the full experience of the exposure, you're reinforcing the idea that you need distraction because you aren't strong enough on your own to endure the experience.

Have Your Avoidance Behaviors Increased?

Now that you have identified the escape, avoidance, procrastination, and safety behaviors associated with your fears, it's time to take a look at how they have increased over time. Use the following worksheet to highlight how these behaviors have increased. First, identify your central fear(s). Then write down your most recent escape, avoidance, procrastination, and safety behaviors associated with that fear. Date them in the next column.

Avoidance Timeline WORKSHEET

FEAR	BEHAVIOR	DATE

As you glance over this last worksheet, notice how your behaviors have slowly come to restrict your activities over time. Ask yourself: Has your anxiety increased, along with the increase in your avoidance behaviors? The answer is probably yes. It's time to eliminate these behaviors, because they make things worse. They're like a wildfire that needs to be put out by cutting the brush and creating fire breaks.

Examine Your Fear Hierarchy

Finally, in the last worksheet before moving on to the exposure exercises, examine what your fears might be if you abandon your various forms of avoidance. The goal of this exercise is to think realistically about taking the first step toward exposure, which is to abandon avoidance.

1. *In the first column, write down your worst fears. Start with the most extreme fear, then go to a lesser fear, and so on.*

2. *Next, in the* Subjective Units of Distress Scale (SUDS) *column, rate each fear according to the severity of distress you feel about it, 100 being the highest, and 1 being the lowest (see page 24).*

3. *Finish the worksheet by filling in the* Forms of Avoidance *and* What Would Occur *columns.*

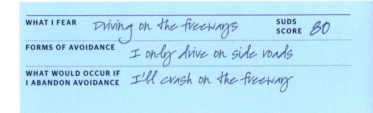

When you come back to this worksheet after you complete the exercises in the next section, you'll be struck by how unfounded your estimates are of what would occur if you abandon the forms of avoidance. Although you understand, now, that everything you have done to avoid anxiety has not worked for you, you have yet to experience the truth in this concept. That's where the exposure exercises come into play.

Fear Hierarchy WORKSHEET

WHAT I FEAR	SUDS SCORE
FORMS OF AVOIDANCE	
WHAT WOULD OCCUR IF I ABANDON AVOIDANCE	

WHAT I FEAR	SUDS SCORE
FORMS OF AVOIDANCE	
WHAT WOULD OCCUR IF I ABANDON AVOIDANCE	

WHAT I FEAR	SUDS SCORE
FORMS OF AVOIDANCE	
WHAT WOULD OCCUR IF I ABANDON AVOIDANCE	

WHAT I FEAR	SUDS SCORE
FORMS OF AVOIDANCE	
WHAT WOULD OCCUR IF I ABANDON AVOIDANCE	

WHAT I FEAR	SUDS SCORE
FORMS OF AVOIDANCE	
WHAT WOULD OCCUR IF I ABANDON AVOIDANCE	

WHAT I FEAR	SUDS SCORE
FORMS OF AVOIDANCE	
WHAT WOULD OCCUR IF I ABANDON AVOIDANCE	

HABIT #2
Learn to Recondition Yourself

If you face your fears, you only need to do it once to retrain your brain.
NO

To deactivate your amygdala, you need to expose yourself to what you fear over and over again.

To recondition yourself, your job will be to avoid avoidance behaviors. You will learn that the amygdala does not lose its fear reactivity easily. You cannot deactivate your amygdala as if turning off a light switch. You must recondition it by exposing yourself repeatedly to what you fear until it becomes innocuous and you habituate to it. Making fear and anxiety go away through what has been called "extinction" (learning that nothing terrible actually happens) requires considerable time and repeated exposure, but it can be done.

The Stubborn Amygdala

The amygdala generalizes what you encounter (it overreacts to anything remotely similar to your initial fear) and does not change its reactivity quickly. Simply deciding to change your anxiety level will not change it. That's only the first step. You need repeated exposures to make new learning possible in the amygdala. Repeated exposures include the fear-triggering stimulus and calming techniques, such as breathing and positive self-talk.

The key to reconditioning is to break the vicious avoidance cycle. You must also make sure that you expose yourself to what you were fearful of in the past. By keeping your behavioral options open to anxiety-provoking experiences, you allow yourself to be flexible and resilient to changing situations. By shifting to exposing yourself to what made you anxious in the past, you can learn to recondition yourself and habituate to that situation, event, or object.

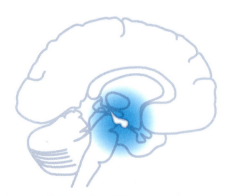

SANDY OVERCOMES HER FEAR OF FLYING

Sandy, a thirty-two-year-old flight attendant, developed a fear of flying after a near collision. To avert a disaster, the pilot abruptly dropped the plane in elevation by 1,000 feet (300 meters).

Sandy had been walking in the aisle at the time and was thrown around the plane like a sack of potatoes. Although she was treated for bruises in the hospital, amazingly, she suffered no broken bones. She felt lucky to be alive. Sandy's face was bruised, however, so the airline gave her a few weeks off to recover. During that time, she and her family were surprised that she suffered no residual stress or nightmares.

Eventually, Sandy got a call from the airline to come back to work. She responded by saying that she wasn't ready to go back to work on an airplane. She offered to work checking in luggage, but the airline management rejected this idea. She responded by having a panic attack. After being given an ultimatum to return to work or be fired, Sandy came in to a mental health department for treatment. She demanded to see a psychiatrist and be given anti-anxiety medication. The psychiatrist gave her a prescription for Ativan.

Not long after the psychiatrist signed her disability forms, Sandy's life began to shrink. She withdrew from her usual range of activities and began to feel anxious about ordinary activities. For example, in addition to her fear of flying, she developed a fear of driving on freeways. Then she became anxious about driving in general. Her psychiatrist became concerned that she was regressing and sent her to an anxiety class.

Sandy said that it was "easier" to avoid anything that made her anxious. But her avoidant behaviors were actually contributing to her anxiety. She would eventually become agoraphobic if she continued to increase them.

The anxious part of her brain, the amygdala, was essentially hijacking her frontal lobes. Because she was withdrawing, rather than confronting, her fears, she was shifting to a right frontal-lobe dominance, with its negative feelings, and underactivating her left frontal lobe, with

CONTINUES NEXT PAGE >

SANDY'S FEAR OF FLYING / CONTINUED >

its positive (can-do) feelings. She needed to take action to activate her left frontal lobe. This description of what was happening in her brain seemed to make sense to her. In fact, she said, "This makes it tangible."

Despite getting the concept down, and developing an exposure plan, Sandy wanted to wait until she was feeling less anxious. But her anxiety would actually increase if she waited; that waiting itself was an avoidant behavior.

Sandy began with driving on the freeway. Her hope was that one time would do it. However, she needed to do it many times to promote neuroplasticity and habituation. Despite her anxiety, she did so while practicing breathing techniques and self-talk.

This exercise helped to reduce her fears, but she still didn't want to approach flying again until she had "built up her confidence." Her therapist convinced her to move forward and they developed a plan for gradual exposure. She began by going to the airport each day. Next, she walked up to the gates to say hello to colleagues. A week after that, with the aid of her colleagues, she entered an airplane. Next, she took a short flight, and then another. Soon, she was ready for a longer flight. All the while, she practiced breathing techniques, self-talk, and mindfulness meditation.

HABIT #3
Practice Exposure and Observation

Exposing yourself to what you fear and observing it, rather resisting the process, makes it easier.
YES

One of the techniques of successful exposure is to accept the experience at all levels. This means that instead of gritting your teeth (a safety behavior), you fully expose yourself to the situation and observe yourself doing it.

This technique allows you to *decenter* the anxiety-provoking effect. You are essentially stepping back from resisting any anxiety and allowing yourself to go through the experience. You're stepping back from the fight. This helps you be a detached observer, rather than a person trying to avoid being anxious.

This may seem like a subtle point. But consider for a moment what happens when you detach and become an observer. Instead of investing your energy in trying to avoid what makes you anxious, you're allowing your observing skills to take center stage. When you're engaging in avoidant behaviors, the anxiety and your avoidance of it takes all your attention. By taking a step back and accepting the experience, you become an observer, which enlarges your perspective. You become more than a person who is trying to stay away from anxiety.

HABIT #4
Practice Real-Life Exposure

You only need to imagine yourself dealing with a situation that creates fear and you'll be able to overcome it.
NO

Real-life exposure is considerably more powerful than imagery exposure.

Sometimes referred to as "in vivo" exposure, real-life exposures involve putting yourself in the situations that you fear. Consider the imagery exercises you just performed as a step toward real-life (in vivo) exposure. In vivo exposure, for example, entails actually approaching a real roomful of people you have never met.

Each time you perform this example exercise, you increase your contact with others. Eventually, you walk up and introduce yourself to someone you don't know. Whatever method you use (imaginary or in vivo), the exposure should be graduated in intensity and never retreating.

Certainly, real-life exposure is more difficult than imagined exposure. It can be difficult even for those without anxiety disorders to face their fears. Try not to get discouraged. In fact, remind yourself while doing the exposure exercises that the more difficulty you have with the exposure exercise, the more effective it will be.

Remember, too, that you have already performed the imagined exercises, so you already have a head start. Take your exposures in steps. Use your worksheet on short-term and long-term goals from chapter 5, and practice setting short-term goals to reach your long-term goal.

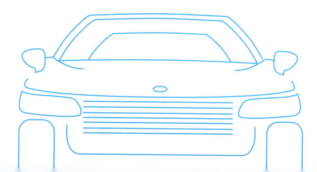

FACING YOUR FEARS

AMANDA SETS GOALS TO OVERCOME HER BRIDGE PHOBIA

Amanda took a job in San Francisco just south of where she lived. Her commute to work included driving across the Golden Gate Bridge daily, which frightened her horribly. The Golden Gate Bridge, in contrast to the other bridges in the Bay Area, features cross traffic, and head-on accidents on the bridge are not uncommon.

Sometimes, these accidents occur when a driver gazes out at the spectacular view or at pedestrians strolling on the walkway and swerves into the oncoming lane. She was afraid to even cross the bridge in the lane furthest away from oncoming traffic so she could enjoy the drive. "I could fall off the side if I was too far over to the right."

Despite her catastrophic thinking, Amanda developed a number of short-term goals in service of her long-term goal of driving across the bridge. To start with, Amanda used imagined exposure, then, after reaching a 20 SUDS score, she moved on to an in vivo exposure.

First, she walked across the bridge until her score went down to a 20 SUDS score. She then graduated to taking a bus, and after reaching a 20 SUDS score at that, she moved on to being a passenger in a car. Finally, she drove across the bridge by herself, repeating the exposure until her SUDS score dropped to 20.

Below is an excerpt from Amanda's exposure worksheet. Her long-term goal is to drive across the Golden Gate Bridge.

Amanda's In Vivo Exposure WORKSHEET

SHORT-TERM GOAL	DRIVING ACROSS THE BRIDGE	
FEAR head-on accident	**SUDS BEFORE EXPOSURE**	80
REALISTIC APPRAISAL i'm in the far right lane and no one can hit me	**SUDS AFTER EXPOSURE**	25

SHORT-TERM GOAL	TAKING A BUS ACROSS BRIDGE	
FEAR the bus will crash	**SUDS BEFORE EXPOSURE**	70
REALISTIC APPRAISAL i'll be safe, even if the improbable happens	**SUDS AFTER EXPOSURE**	15

SHORT-TERM GOAL	WALKING ACROSS THE BRIDGE	
FEAR someone will push me over	**SUDS BEFORE EXPOSURE**	65
REALISTIC APPRAISAL noone is stupid enough to try	**SUDS AFTER EXPOSURE**	10

Identify Your Short-Term and Long-Term Exposure Goals

Use the following worksheet to monitor your graduated and sequential exposures. Just like Amanda, structure your short-term exposure goals, so they lead you to accomplish your long-term goal. After your SUDS score goes down to 20, move to the next short-term goal (a more difficult exposure). Be sure to reach a 20 SUDS score before going to the next short-term exposure goal (see page 24).

In Vivo Exposure WORKSHEET

SHORT-TERM GOAL

FEAR

SUDS BEFORE
EXPOSURE

REALISTIC APPRAISAL

SUDS AFTER
EXPOSURE

SHORT-TERM GOAL

FEAR

SUDS BEFORE
EXPOSURE

REALISTIC APPRAISAL

SUDS AFTER
EXPOSURE

SHORT-TERM GOAL

FEAR

SUDS BEFORE
EXPOSURE

REALISTIC APPRAISAL

SUDS AFTER
EXPOSURE

SHORT-TERM GOAL

FEAR

SUDS BEFORE
EXPOSURE

REALISTIC APPRAISAL

SUDS AFTER
EXPOSURE

SHORT-TERM GOAL

FEAR

SUDS BEFORE
EXPOSURE

REALISTIC APPRAISAL

SUDS AFTER
EXPOSURE

STEVEN USES EXPOSURE TO EXPAND HIS WORLD

Steven had been married for six years and had a four-year-old son. Over the past few years, Steven was gradually withdrawing to limit his activities to home and work. It was only after his wife threatened to leave him because he wanted to quit his job that he sought help.

Steven had always been a worrier, but, in recent years, he found that the number of situations that made him feel overwhelmingly anxious had grown. He withdrew in response to this increase in anxiety. At work, he sometimes got up abruptly and left a meeting if he felt anxious. Often, he avoided going into the conference room or break room, for fear of getting involved in a conversation. Some of his peers had begun to say, "What's up, Steve?" He didn't know what to say.

After a few weeks of practicing the skills you're learning, Steven found that his general level of free-floating anxiety had subsided. As a first step toward the exposure exercise, he completed the work-sheets on identifying his escape, avoidant, procrastination, and safety behaviors. He was amazed by how many he had and how they had increased over time. Next, he began the imagined exposures, followed by the in vivo exercises.

Steven started his exposure exercises by imagining going into the break room at work. First, he simply stood there and listened to others. Then, he imagined striking up a conversation. He followed the imagined exercise with real-life exposure by first entering the break room, then approaching one of his colleagues to ask a question, then finally striking up a conversation.

Over the next few weeks, Steven worked hard to develop new behaviors that surprised his coworkers. And he was delighted to report that his wife praised him for saying that he intended to stick it out at work.

HABIT #5
Practice Increasing Your Exposure Intensity (Imagined and In Vivo)

Gradually exposing yourself to what you fear will reduce your anxiety over time.
YES

Gradually increasing your exposure through your imagination and in real life will reduce your anxiety over time.

Use the following worksheet to chart the progress of your exposures. Write down the type of exposure in the first column (note whether it is imagined or in vivo), then note the symptoms you experienced. Next, give yourself a SUDS score and describe the coping techniques you used. Finally, write down your plan for the next exposure.

For this exposure, increase the time period or the intensity of it. The point here is that you want to dose yourself with ever-increasing amounts of what you had found intolerable in the past. For example, let's return to Amanda's bridge phobia. With imagined exposure, she can have the traffic come to a halt, or she can turn around and drive back over the bridge again. In fact, Amanda did turn around after crossing the bridge and drove across again. This helped her habituate to the experience of driving across the bridge. The more she did it, the more at ease she was the next time. Perform your exposures until your SUDS goes down to 20 (see page 24). Then increase the intensity and repeat the exposure until your SUDS again goes down to 20. Each time, note the coping skills that you used and the plan to modify those coping skills for the next exposure.

SUDS Exposure WORKSHEET

TYPE OF EXPOSURE   **SUDS**

SYMPTOMS

COPING SKILL

PLAN FOR THE NEXT EXPOSURE

TYPE OF EXPOSURE   **SUDS**

SYMPTOMS

COPING SKILL

PLAN FOR THE NEXT EXPOSURE

TYPE OF EXPOSURE   **SUDS**

SYMPTOMS

COPING SKILL

PLAN FOR THE NEXT EXPOSURE

Notice how the symptoms change with each exposure. Similarly, watch how your SUDS score changes. At the end of the sheet, you'll notice that, although the intensities of the exposures increased, your SUDS score eventually decreased. This exercise represents a fundamental truth about anxiety: The more you expose yourself to the things and situations you fear, the less anxiety you will suffer. Because avoidant behaviors increase your anxiety, your treatment should include exposure. There is no way to escape this fact, so practice the exercises in this chapter often.

Accepting Your Bodily Sensations

07

Learning to sit with anxiety is one of the most difficult things to do. Does it make you feel better or worse?

Take the quiz and find out how to accept your bodily sensations in this chapter >

TRUE

FALSE

(T) (F) *Trying to ignore or suppress feelings of anxiety makes them go away faster.*

(T) (F) *You can learn to be comfortable with uncomfortable sensations.*

(T) (F) *Creating sensations of anxiety can help you accept them rather than fear them.*

(T) (F) *Practicing feeling anxious just makes you more anxious.*

Learning to Not Fear Feeling

In the preceding chapters, you learned that mistaken beliefs frame what you avoid with fear and that avoidance behaviors lead to more anxiety. You learned how to change your mistaken beliefs, avoid avoidance, and make exposure to things you fear a habit. Now, you're ready to take the next step. You will actually induce some of the physical sensations associated with anxiety and panic so that you can habituate to them and neutralize their negative effects.

Because you have been working to change your automatic thoughts, assumptions, and core beliefs and have learned relaxation exercises, as well as breathing and positive self-talk, you're now better able to cope with and adapt to the physical sensations you overreacted to in the past.

Your new thinking skills have helped you understand that your physical sensations are nothing to be alarmed about. Now, your thoughts and emotions need to be integrated positively with your physical sensations. Because your thoughts often lead the way, and your emotions eventually follow, integrating positive thoughts are important when experiencing the bodily sensations you have been avoiding like the plague.

In this chapter, you'll learn the skills necessary to accept the physical sensations associated with anxiety and panic so that they can fade into the background and won't continue to demand your attention. You'll learn:

- *Why it's important to face your physical sensations*

- *That your physical sensations are not dangerous*

- *How overreacting to physical sensations leads to panic*

- *How to break the panic cycle by riding out the physical sensations*

- *How to use interoceptive exposure to habituate to your physical sensations*

What Is Anxiety Sensitivity?

One of the factors that contributes to avoidant behaviors is referred to as "anxiety sensitivity." If you think that any anxiety is bad and must be avoided, you cultivate anxiety sensitivity—you become hypersensitive to the sensations that you assume signal danger ahead. They are actually false alarms.

Here's how it works: Let's say you are anxious in social situations. You decide that you will engage in social situations only when you are free of anxiety, because you don't want others to know that you are anxious. Each time you experience some anxiety, you experience it in an all-or-nothing way.

Although there are actually degrees of anxiety, when you're stuck in an all-or-nothing mode, a little feels like a lot. A little anxiety in a social situation becomes intolerable, because even a little anxiety is too much to handle. So you avoid similar situations. Then other situations that are the slightest bit social make you anxious, just by thinking about them.

Soon the physical sensations that you associate with anxiety occur without provocation. When you try to avoid those sensations, your anxiety sensitivity increases. And, most important, your anxiety level increases because you fear the physical sensations.

Why It's Important to Recognize False Alarms

Dr. David Barlow from Boston University pointed out the importance of differentiating between false alarms and real alarms. False alarms are learned (conditioned) alarms. A false alarm is like Doug's feeling of tightness in his chest. When he felt his chest become tight, the alarm went off that something terrible was going to happen, and he began to panic. But nothing terrible did happen. So the alarm wasn't real. When you avoid dealing with learned alarms, they can strengthen and become resistant to extinction.

DOUG'S ANXIETY SENSITIVITY

Doug's symptoms of anxiety included feeling a tightness in his chest and some constriction in his throat. When he felt these sensations, he began to have trouble swallowing and began to breathe quickly. Pretty soon, his heart started to race and he began to panic. Because of this, Doug began to monitor and fear feeling tightness in his chest.

Over time, even a little tightness became too much tightness. He did whatever he could to minimize any chance of feeling this sensation. Doug's sensitivity made his anxiety worse.

HABIT #1
Become More Comfortable in Your Body

Trying to ignore or suppress feelings of anxiety makes them go away faster.
FALSE

Trying to suppress anxiety makes it worse.

A paradox occurs when you try to avoid your physical sensations. When you try really hard *not* to feel something, you'll feel it even more. For example, try really hard not to notice your anxiety.
Try to block out those sensations! Doing so makes you notice them even more, right? But a funny thing happens when you stop trying. Once you acknowledge and simply observe the sensations of the anxiety, they fade into the background. This is the principle used in many chronic pain programs. Chronic pain patients learn to stop trying to avoid or block out the physical sensations of pain and instead observe and accept them. This can be frightening for people who have been traumatized by debilitating pain.

Why face terrible pain when they have had too much of it already? The answer is that by accepting the pain, it actually fades. This is one step toward making chronic pain tolerable. The same principle applies to the physical sensations you associate with anxiety. You want to stop trying *not* to feel those sensations. Instead, observe and accept them.

HABIT #2
Desensitize Yourself to Bodily Sensations

You can learn to be comfortable with uncomfortable sensations.
TRUE

Using interoceptive exposure can help you be more comfortable with the symptoms of anxiety.

Now that you understand detached-observer perspective and deconditioning, let's talk about a technique called "interoceptive exposure," which will help you habituate to your own bodily sensations so that they won't frighten you.

Interoceptive and Extroceptive Fear

There are two main sources of fear that generate anxiety disorders: *extroceptive* and *interoceptive*. Extroceptive fear is about something outside of you. Interoceptive fear is about something inside of you.

Extroceptive fear occurs when you overreact to feared objects or situations. For example, in social phobia, extroceptive fear occurs when you stand in front of a group of people, giving a presentation. Interoceptive fear refers to your reactions to internal sensations, such as the physical sensations that occur when you stand in front of those people: a dry mouth, sweating, and butterflies in your stomach.

Interoceptive exposure is a process of systematically desensitizing yourself to those physical sensations; it helps you habituate to them. During interoceptive exposure, you restructure your thinking, using positive self-talk and narratives, while experiencing the physical sensations that arise. Developing new automatic thoughts and assumptions during interoceptive exposure exercises helps you gain confidence and learn to ride out those physical sensations, so they eventually become innocuous.

Remember, the goal is not to eliminate anxiety but to reduce it and make it more manageable. Anxiety is a necessary part of life that can be used to keep you constructively alert and motivated.

Cultivating the Right Mindset to Become More Comfortable in Your Own Skin

Normally, a person without PD appraises activated physical sensations, such as rapid heartbeat and shortness of breath, as innocuous. A realistic assessment of the potential danger of an anxiety-provoking situation derails the fight-or-flight response from being triggered. The brain's hippocampus accesses memories and context that allow for such thoughts as, "Oh yes, I've had shortness of breath and a rapid heartbeat before. Nothing bad happened."

Some researchers, including Dr. Albert Bandura of Stanford University, have pointed out that believing in your ability to succeed is the most important factor operating in anxiety disorders. If you think that you are unable to cope with anxiety in what you assume to be a potentially threatening situation, your anxiety increases.

When you develop self-confidence, your anxiety decreases. In other words, when you believe that you are able to deal with the situation, your anxiety level goes down. When you observe and accept the physical sensations that arise, your sense of mastery over them makes your anxiety fade.

Bandura cites well-known studies that involved administering epinephrine (adrenaline) to subjects who were led to believe that they were either in a positive (controllable) or negative (uncontrollable) situation. Those who believed that they were in an uncontrollable situation experienced increased anxiety from the epinephrine. Those who were led to believe that they were in a controllable situation reported great pleasure. The point is that a shot of adrenaline doesn't necessarily lead to anxiety. It's all in how you interpret the sensations. If you interpret the physical sensations positively, or at least as a neutral experience, you won't be plagued by anxiety. If your previous response to the physical sensations was to avoid them, this may seem like strange advice.

But if you invite, accept, and do not resist your physical sensations, you will defuse, disarm, and diminish their negative effect. It means learning to do the opposite of what you feel is safe.

What Are Your Current Automatic Physical Sensations?

As a first step toward learning interoceptive exposure, let's examine your current automatic physical sensations. In the left-hand column, write down the physical sensations that apply to you. These physical sensations can include sweaty palms, rapid heartbeat, and shallow breathing, among others. In the right-hand column, write down your usual response to these sensations.

Assess Your Physical Sensations WORKSHEET

PHYSICAL SENSATIONS	RESPONSES
Shortness of breath	I breathe harder to get more air

Identify Your Coping Skills

Now that you've assessed what your usual responses are to physical sensations, it's time to practice your coping skills. Use the following worksheet to identify the physical sensations and the newly learned skills you will use to cope with each one. This exercise will help you remember to use your coping skills.

Identify Your Coping Skills WORKSHEET

PHYSICAL SENSATIONS	RESPONSES
Shortness of breath	I'll breathe abdominally

HABIT #3
Practice Your Coping Skills

Creating sensations of anxiety can help you accept them rather than fear them.
TRUE

Coping skills can help you to move toward, not away from, the physical sensations that make you anxious.

You'll do this by creating anxiety and practicing coping skills to help you deal with the physical sensations that you don't like. This probably sounds like a frightening challenge but remember that rewiring your brain requires that you do what you don't want to do to create new habits. Remember, if you do what you feel like doing, you'll continue strengthening old habits. You generally do what comes easily, and the more you do those things, the more you will do them again and the more they will eventually come easily. Change requires forcing yourself to establish new habits, especially when your old habits include avoiding discomfort.

Prepare for the Exercises

In the following pages, you will be using a variety of methods to induce the physical sensations you fear. It's time to gain mastery over these false alarms. You'll soon learn to habituate to the physical symptoms to which you've been overreacting.

Before you get started, check out this list. Some things are useful to have available for the exercises, while others are things to keep in mind as you prepare for the exercises:

- *Use the worksheets in this chapter to help demonstrate gains as you practice the interoceptive exposure exercises. In addition to the worksheets, you might need the following items: a timer, a pencil, and a straw.*

- *There is a major difference between anxiety and sensation intensity: Anxiety is uncomfortable at best and frightening at worst; sensation intensity (shortness of breath and dizziness) need only be uncomfortable at its worst. To see this difference, observe your SUDS score go down, despite the physical discomfort.*

- *Some people like to have a coach available (a friend or family member) to give encouragement. You may want the coach to do the exercises with you.*

- *It's common to experience anxiety or panic the first few times you perform the exercises. This a great opportunity to practice the anxiety-reduction techniques you learned in the previous chapters. You need practice!*

- *Allow yourself to fully experience the symptoms. Trust your ability to succeed. The idea is to habituate to the sensations. You want the full benefit of the exposure.*

- *The exposures should be regular and graduated in intensity. In other words, you'll need to do them often and increase the difficulty level steadily. Don't practice sporadically, and then try to make up for lost time by ratcheting up the intensity too quickly.*

- *Apply coping skills, such as abdominal breathing and positive self-talk, during the exposure exercises. Say to yourself, "Oh, this rapid heartbeat is no big thing. I've experienced it many times, and nothing terrible happened."*

- *Stay focused to maximize the involvement of your frontal lobes and memory, so you can allow yourself to increase self-efficacy during the exposure. Pay attention and observe yourself as you perform the exposure.*

The interoceptive exercises include:

Over-breathing	**Shaking your head from side to side**
Holding your breath	
Tensing your body	**Putting your head between your legs, then sitting up**
Staring at one spot	

Caution:

There are a few exclusions for these exercises. If you are pregnant or have asthma, a heart condition, low blood pressure, or epilepsy, don't engage in these exercises.

Ask your doctor whether these exercises put your medical situation at risk.

Track Your Progress

The worksheets that follow on pages 126 to 131 are designed to track your progress and to show you how you can improve. Each of the exposures, such as spinning or over-breathing, should be performed repeatedly and as instructed. Don't forget that the physical symptoms are not dangerous! Getting your heart rate up will not cause a heart attack; hyperventilating will not cause you to pass out; and swallowing quickly won't make you choke to death. For each worksheet:

- *Jot down your symptoms. Give them a SUDS score (see page 24).*

- *Write down your worst fear(s). Estimate the odds they'll happen.*

- *Note whether your worst fear occurred: Yes or No.*

- *Write down what you did to cope.*

Your goal is to repeat each exercise until your SUDS score goes down to 20. Don't try to do them all in one day all at once. Try each of these exercises over several weeks.

Over-Breathing Exercise

Over-breathing leads to lightheadedness and rapid heartbeat. This over-breathing exercise can illustrate how to unlink hyperventilation and panic. Your task is to hyperventilate by breathing quickly, with an emphasis on the exhale, for 1½ minutes. Alternatively, you can breathe through a straw for 1 minute. Hold your nose while breathing through the straw and try to get as much air as you can.

Over-Breathing WORKSHEET

TRIAL 01

YOUR SYMPTOMS   SUDS

WORST FEAR   DID IT HAPPEN?

YOUR COPING SKILLS

TRIAL 02

YOUR SYMPTOMS   SUDS

WORST FEAR   DID IT HAPPEN?

YOUR COPING SKILLS

TRIAL 03

YOUR SYMPTOMS   SUDS

WORST FEAR   DID IT HAPPEN?

YOUR COPING SKILLS

Carol described her physical symptoms after the over-breathing exercise like this: "That got my heart racing, and my mind was right behind it." She also said that she started sweating and felt dizzy. Her hands shook, and her throat went dry. She gave it a 98 on the SUDS for the first trial. During trial #2, it went down to 81. Her mind did not race, but her heart rate remained high. After trial #3, her SUDS score went down to 63. She was amazed that it was getting easier. On trial #5, she said, "I'm getting the hang of it now. I'd say this is a 20. Maybe less!"

Holding Your Breath Exercise

Hold your breath for 30 seconds. This tightens the chest and leads to a sense of suffocation. This exercise probably sounds like an odd one to induce the physical sensations associated with anxious feelings. But tightness in your chest and the accompanying sense of suffocation can cause you to gasp for air and begin to breathe quickly to compensate. This can lead to a variety of symptoms that can trigger a false alarm and cascade into panic. By practicing this exposure, you can shift this sensation from being a trigger for a panic attack to simply an innocuous sensation.

Breath-Holding WORKSHEET

TRIAL 01

YOUR SYMPTOMS

SUDS

WORST FEAR

DID IT HAPPEN?

YOUR COPING SKILLS

TRIAL 02

YOUR SYMPTOMS

SUDS

WORST FEAR

DID IT HAPPEN?

YOUR COPING SKILLS

TRIAL 03

YOUR SYMPTOMS

SUDS

WORST FEAR

DID IT HAPPEN?

YOUR COPING SKILLS

After holding her breath for trial #1, Carol said, "That forced me to start breathing fast, and that got my heart pumping, too!" She rated it an 80 and worried that she had damaged her lungs. Trial #2 was easier. She didn't resort to breathing quickly, and her heart rate was stable. For trial #3, she decided to see whether she could hold her breath for longer than the 30 seconds. Her SUDS score rose to 80. She was quite relieved when her SUDS score for the next few trials dropped quickly.

Body Tension Exercise

While sitting, tense your entire body, making fists and bringing your shoulders forward. Tighten your chest and entire body. Body tension can trigger a false alarm because during periods of anxiety your body can tense up. The associations that you make when you tense up can unconsciously remind you of feeling anxious, but they need not lead to anxiety. In this exercise, you'll learn to make sure that they don't.

Body Tension WORKSHEET

TRIAL 01

YOUR SYMPTOMS

SUDS

WORST FEAR

DID IT HAPPEN?

YOUR COPING SKILLS

TRIAL 02

YOUR SYMPTOMS

SUDS

WORST FEAR

DID IT HAPPEN?

YOUR COPING SKILLS

TRIAL 03

YOUR SYMPTOMS

SUDS

WORST FEAR

DID IT HAPPEN?

YOUR COPING SKILLS

Carol said, "Oh, I don't know how I'm going to get my body any tenser." Her worst fear was that she would make her muscles spasm, then have a heart attack or seizures and die. She rated trial #1 at 95. "I felt like my body locked up! Why did I have to do that?" She was able to loosen up after a few moments of constricted breathing and feeling that she was trapped in her own body. After trials #2, #3, #4, and #5, she loosened up more quickly and rated her SUDS at 80, 71, 50, and 33, respectively. She said, "You know, that's a funny way to relax. I think I'll do it more often."

Staring Exercise

Pick a spot on a blank wall and stare at it without deviation for 2 minutes. This can simulate the feeling of being trapped. Those with claustrophobia might find this exercise particularly troublesome. Try to keep at it, though; in the long run, it can help you lessen the effects of claustrophobia. The feeling of being confused and trapped can trigger anxiety and the need to look away as a means to calm yourself down. Resist this temptation. Remember you want to stir up disturbing sensations, so that you can eventually habituate to them.

Staring WORKSHEET

TRIAL 01

YOUR SYMPTOMS   SUDS

WORST FEAR   DID IT HAPPEN?

YOUR COPING SKILLS

TRIAL 02

YOUR SYMPTOMS   SUDS

WORST FEAR   DID IT HAPPEN?

YOUR COPING SKILLS

TRIAL 03

YOUR SYMPTOMS   SUDS

WORST FEAR   DID IT HAPPEN?

YOUR COPING SKILLS

The idea of staring at a spot on the wall as an anxiety exercise struck Carol as a joke. However, as she was getting ready to do it, she realized that she couldn't look away. She reflected anxiously for a moment. "What if something happens?" She rated trial #1 an 87 on the SUDS scale. She reported that her heart started racing, and she started hyperventilating. On trial #2, she found herself beginning to relax. Her SUDS score went down to 70. By trial #4, she was down to 20 with no symptoms and said, "That was kind of a meditative exercise."

Shaking Your Head Exercise

Set a timer for 1½ minutes. Shake your head from side to side. Lower your head and shift it from side to side. When the timer goes off after 1½ minutes, raise your head. This exercise is similar to the standing-up exercise in that one of the most common symptoms is dizziness, followed by blurry vision. Think of it as a good neck exercise, but do it slowly so you don't pull a muscle. Don't forget that you want to induce uncomfortable sensations so that you can habituate to them.

Shaking Your Head WORKSHEET

TRIAL 01

YOUR SYMPTOMS

SUDS

WORST FEAR

DID IT HAPPEN?

YOUR COPING SKILLS

TRIAL 02

YOUR SYMPTOMS

SUDS

WORST FEAR

DID IT HAPPEN?

YOUR COPING SKILLS

TRIAL 03

YOUR SYMPTOMS

SUDS

WORST FEAR

DID IT HAPPEN?

YOUR COPING SKILLS

Carol found this exercise distracting. In fact, after trial #1, Carol reported both blurry vision and dizziness. She rated it a SUDS of 83. By trial #4, she was down to a 20 rating on the SUDS scale.

Head Between Your Legs Exercise

Sit in a straight-backed chair and put your head between your legs. Make sure that your head is below your heart. After 1 minute, sit up straight. Like the standing up exercise, this creates an abrupt change in the blood flow to your head, resulting in lightheadedness, blurry vision, and a little dizziness.

Head Between Your Legs WORKSHEET

TRIAL 01

YOUR SYMPTOMS	SUDS

WORST FEAR	DID IT HAPPEN?

YOUR COPING SKILLS

TRIAL 02

YOUR SYMPTOMS	SUDS

WORST FEAR	DID IT HAPPEN?

YOUR COPING SKILLS

TRIAL 03

YOUR SYMPTOMS	SUDS

WORST FEAR	DID IT HAPPEN?

YOUR COPING SKILLS

This exercise made Carol laugh. "You gotta be kidding! What does this have to do with anxiety?" But after trial #1, she felt lightheaded and dizzy. She said, "My heart skipped a beat! That was a 90." But she rated trial #6 a 15.

HABIT #4
Practice Interoceptive Exposure Whenever You Feel Anxious

Practicing feeling anxious just makes you more anxious.
FALSE

Practicing inducing the symptoms of anxiety can help you better cope with things you don't expect.

You'll have plenty of opportunities for interoceptive exposure when you don't plan it. The physical sensations you feared can still occur spontaneously. When they do, you will probably feel a little more anxious. That's okay, and it's expected. You can now react to them as false alarms.

Consider spontaneous events as opportunities to practice your new counter-conditioning skills. You'll get better at dealing with them as you practice inducing the symptoms. The more you practice, the more prepared you'll be to derail a potential panic attack. By practicing the interoceptive exposure exercises with the techniques you have learned in the preceding chapters, your panic attacks will begin to fade away.

MAKE IT A HABIT

These exercises should be practiced regularly, especially if you have suffered from panic attacks. Practicing rewires your brain to establish new healthy habits.

Part Three

Managing Relapses and Setbacks

Whenever you begin to adopt new habits to improve your life, it's normal for there to be relapses and setbacks. After all, you're human, not a robot, and no one does everything perfectly. Relapses and setbacks can actually be useful because they can help you identify problem areas and enable you to make changes to help you deal with your anxiety more effectively. In Part Three, you'll discover how to minimize the possibility of a setback and keep moving forward by adopting habits like self-care, labeling what can make you anxious, and dealing with triggers. You'll also learn how to deal with a setback when (and if) it happens, how to get back on track, and integrate relapse-prevention skills into your daily life. All of these habits will help you manage anxiety more effectively and enjoy life more.

Preventing Relapse

08

When you adopt new habits and begin to make progress, it's common to have setbacks. But when it comes to anxiety, do you know what can and can't help you stay anxiety free?

Take the quiz to find out >

TRUE

FALSE

(T) (F) *Making self-care a priority can minimize the odds of an anxiety flare-up.*

(T) (F) *To avoid setbacks, it's important to identify situations that may trigger anxiety in the future and plan for them.*

(T) (F) *It's better to use avoidance behavior than to keep exposing yourself to things that make you anxious.*

(T) (F) *Once you're free of anxiety, you'll never feel it again.*

(T) (F) *Getting over a setback means going back to anxiety practices that worked for you before.*

(T) (F) *Being assertive reduces anxiety because it makes you feel in control.*

(T) (F) *It's okay to have some weak coping skills because your strong skills will balance them out.*

(T) (F) *A relapse-prevention plan gives you the foundation you need to keep your anxiety recovery on track, no matter what happens.*

HABIT #1
Practice Good Self-Care

Making self-care a priority can minimize the odds of an anxiety flare-up.
TRUE

One of the best ways to minimize your vulnerability to anxiety symptoms is to practice good self-care. You want your brain and the rest of your body to be fit.

Consume a healthy diet. Consuming a diet that includes too much sugar, caffeine, and unbalanced meals can promote a neurochemistry that simulates anxiety. Such a diet makes you vulnerable to inducing anxiety symptoms such as rapid heartbeat, sweating, insomnia, light-headedness, shakiness, and shortness of breath. Remember to eat at least three balanced meals a day.

Avoid alcohol and other drugs. Alcohol and other drugs create an imbalance in your neurochemistry that lasts for days and even weeks after your last drink. Also, the day after consuming alcohol (even though the quantity may not be great), you'll be dehydrated.

Stay adequately hydrated. Dehydration contributes to feeling uneasy. Because you are more than 80 percent water, dehydration compromises your body, including your brain cells. When your brain cells are compromised, you're less likely to cope with stress and more likely to feel anxious.

Get enough sleep. Sleep loss makes it more difficult to concentrate, increases your emotional liability, and decreases your ability to deal with stress. If you lose sleep, you may have symptoms such as lightheadedness, shakiness, and feeling tense.

Learn to deal with stress. Stress can destabilize your capacity to function properly, wear you down, and make you more vulnerable to developing symptoms of anxiety. Stress in itself is not a bad thing. In fact, stress is a fact of life, and you don't want to avoid tasks just because they are stressful. It's how you deal with stress that determines the degree of vulnerability to anxiety. Regular practice of coping skills, including the anxiety-reduction techniques you learned, will minimize stress and anxiety.

Avoid multitasking. As you learned earlier, making thinking errors can inadvertently promote anxiety, and you are more likely to make thinking errors if you multitask. This is because it's hard to sort out all your thoughts and feelings when you are shifting from task to task. There's a risk that your scattered thoughts and feelings can add up to feeling overwhelmed. Your thinking then shifts to globalizing—lumping everything together. Multitasking, therefore, promotes stress and then anxiety.

Multitasking includes talking on your cell phone, instant messaging, and text messaging while you are engaging in important activities, like driving, including in difficult traffic. Don't do it! Multitasking like this causes accidents.

Seek social support. Humans are social creatures, so getting support from your close friends and relatives and a partner or spouse can be a great antidote to stress and anxiety. When those relationships are thrown into doubt, such as after a major argument, you can be more vulnerable to experiencing a relapse of anxiety. If you can't resolve the situation with the person, seek out social support from close friends or your spouse to buffer the residual effects of the conflict.

DAWN LEARNS TO MINIMIZE HER MULTITASKING

Dawn rear-ended a car at a stop light because she had been talking on her cell phone while driving. Fortunately, the collision caused no injuries, but it certainly did cause a jump in her insurance premiums and her anxiety. After attending an anxiety class for several weeks, she said she had learned a lot, but that she couldn't give up one bad habit. Although she hated to admit it, she was addicted to multitasking. She rationalized it by saying, "I can get more done than most people." But because of the accident, she agreed to stop using her cell phone while driving.

Dawn's problems resurfaced when she hit a snag with one of her tasks and tumbled into a panic attack. Instead of shifting her attention solely to the problem that needed resolving, she continued to try and juggle all the balls at once—but it wasn't working.

She realized that it was time to develop a contingency strategy. Although she was unwilling to give up multitasking entirely, she did agree that when she ran into a problem with one of her tasks, she would postpone her involvement on the others until the snag was worked through. This contingency strategy helped derail a panic attack before it happened.

HABIT #2
Identify Your Anxiety Triggers

To avoid setbacks, it's important to identify situations that may trigger anxiety in the future and plan for them.
TRUE

It's important to know what triggers your anxiety so that you can plan for and deal with stressful situations.

You can minimize your vulnerability to anxiety, but various situations that triggered anxiety in the past, such as being in a rainstorm or having trouble in a relationship, can occur again. The road to recovery is littered with obstacles, bumps, and potholes in the form of stressful situations that can trigger anxiety. This means that setbacks can occur. Your challenge is to see these setbacks as mere bumps on the road. When you are driving down a road and your car hits a pothole, you don't pull over and say to yourself, "I can't do this! The road is too rough!" You simply acknowledge that there are potholes and adjust your speed accordingly.

Don't Avoid Real-Life Exposure to What You Fear

When you hold on to avoidant behaviors, such as avoiding driving because of potholes, you increase the likelihood of relapse. Relapse prevention should include continual real-life exposure to habituate you to situations you fear. Expose yourself to the situation in which the fear originated. By experiencing repeated exposures to the initial fear-provoking situation, you can form new associations to it. Also, you can develop positive self-talk to disprove your anxiety-provoking predictions of danger.

ANNA DEVELOPS NEW ASSOCIATIONS

Anna developed free-floating anxiety with periodic panic attacks after being harassed at work. She filed a grievance, then quit. Although she found another job, her anxiety and panic attacks continued. She later got help for her anxiety, which helped, but she still avoided driving on the road near her previous place of employment. In fact, she went out of her way to avoid it. By using anxiety-reduction techniques and exposure exercises, she developed a different association to the road and eventually was able to drive on it.

The new associations were formed by having her stop at a grocery store located on the road. She actually went out of her way to get to that store to shop, so that she could recondition herself. Even after she developed a new association to the road, she periodically shopped at the store near her former place of employment, "just to stay in practice."

As you develop your relapse plan, keep in mind the context in which your anxiety is prone to occur. Think of the context as filled with cues that trigger your anxious reactions. Anxiety cues are like signals that alert you that something dangerous is coming. The problem is that many are false alarms.

Katie, for example, had a tendency to feel intimidated by people who expressed thought-provoking opinions and reacted by being overwhelmed with anxiety. Those types of people became the cues that triggered her anxiety.

By working through the exercises and practices in this book, she learned to convert these cues into a positive. Instead of responding with anxiety, she now responds with curiosity and seeks them out to hear their opinions.

What Unique Cues Trigger Your Anxiety?

Use the worksheet below to note the cues that trigger your anxiety, the symptoms that develop, your SUDS score (see page 24), the old coping skills that you used, the skills you forgot to use, and the plan to modify your coping techniques. You'll see Katie's responses as an example. Jot down your unique details and give a lot of thought to what coping skills you forgot and your planning for next time.

Cues Planning WORKSHEET

CUES Intimidating people   **SYMPTOMS** Sweating   **SUDS** 85

OLD COPING SKILLS Leaving the room   **WHAT I FORGOT TO DO** Positive self-talk

MY PLANNING Stay in the room and ask a question

CUES   **SYMPTOMS**   **SUDS**

OLD COPING SKILLS   **WHAT I FORGOT TO DO**

MY PLANNING

CUES   **SYMPTOMS**   **SUDS**

OLD COPING SKILLS   **WHAT I FORGOT TO DO**

MY PLANNING

CUES   **SYMPTOMS**   **SUDS**

OLD COPING SKILLS   **WHAT I FORGOT TO DO**

MY PLANNING

HABIT #3
Avoid Avoidance and Expose Yourself to Anxiety-Provoking Cues

It's better to use avoidance behavior than to keep exposing yourself to things that make you anxious.

FALSE

It's critical to avoid avoidance behaviors and to expose yourself consistently to those remaining anxiety-provoking cues so that they no longer trigger anxiety.

Your long-term plan must entail consistent exposure to the context of the cues that you were avoiding. By exposing yourself to these cues long after your anxiety has faded, you can continue to habituate to them, and you'll engender a sense of durability that can help you when you encounter these cues in the future. This is because the cues that provoke anxiety will become a mere memory. They don't trigger anxiety anymore, because you have made them innocuous. When you continue to expose yourself to them, you keep them converted.

The conversion of cues that trigger anxiety to simple memories provides a vantage point from which you can recognize that many cues and anxiety triggers are arbitrary. Many were associated with anxiety only in your mind. Those cues can as easily be associated with neutral, or even positive, feelings. Your job is to identify those cues and convert them into neutral or positive feelings. This conversion can only be accomplished by continual exposure.

HABIT #4
Learn How to Manage Setbacks without Overreacting

Once you're free of anxiety, you'll never feel it again.
FALSE

It's quite common to experience brief periods of anxiety during and after the recovery process.

Almost no one is anxiety free. This is because anxiety is a good thing. The question is how much you have and how overwhelming it is for you. Your anxiety was not useful to you in the past, and your job now is to make it normal. Unfortunately, it's also quite common for people to get so excited about their progress that they gravitate back to all-or-nothing thinking. Fueled by enthusiasm, they assume that they have been "cured" and that they are completely anxiety free. Once they've made this thinking error, they're at risk of experiencing minor setbacks with periods of disturbing anxiety and falling back into their old pattern of overreacting to the anxiety.

What was once a little anxiety is interpreted as a great deal of anxiety. They assume that they are back to square one, that all the progress they made is lost, and that they have to start all over again. Worse, some people think of themselves as incapable of making *any* long-term progress. Here are common overreactions to setbacks:

- *Why try if I'm just going to fall back again?*
- *After all the work I've done, I'm right back where I started from.*
- *I knew I was incapable of making it last.*
- *This must mean that my anxiety problem is worse than I thought.*
- *Maybe I should go back to avoiding things that make me anxious.*
- *I guess the gains I made were all superficial.*
- *All those anxiety-reduction techniques weren't for people with deep problems like mine.*
- *I can't change my anxiety genes.*
- *Everything I've done is lost now, and I can't climb back up.*
- *All those techniques were just distractions from my real problem.*
- *I might as well just go on medication.*

Other overreactions to setbacks can include:

- *My mother taught me how to be anxious all the time. I guess I should expect it.*
- *I've got a rare anxiety condition and will never be free of terrible anxiety.*
- *Medical marijuana is the answer.*
- *This relapse proves I've got bad brain chemistry.*
- *I guess I've got brain damage, after all.*
- *God forgets to help me sometimes.*

Remember, setbacks are opportunities to learn lessons. They remind you that you weren't practicing your coping skills and that there's still work to be done. They let you know that you have not been following the plan. Rather than overreact, try to view your setback more realistically. Here are some realistic responses to a setback:

- *I guess I was forgetting to take care of myself.*
- *I better practice my coping techniques more often.*
- *I was getting too lazy.*
- *Whoops. I let myself get out of shape.*
- *That was a good reminder to stay with my plan.*
- *I should see one task through, rather than lumping everything together.*
- *There's something to learn from this.*
- *Nobody said it would be easy.*
- *I'll hang in there long-term because of my kids.*
- *It's like I'm training for a long-distance run. I'll pace myself.*
- *I do too much for other people and not enough for myself.*
- *I'm going to find my groove again.*
- *Time to get back into balance once again.*
- *I will reinstall the shock absorbers.*
- *Time to snap out of that fear jag.*
- *My anxiety habit took years to develop, so it'll take a while to unlearn.*
- *I'm not a computer that can be instantaneously reprogrammed.*

Worry Can Lead to a Setback

Worrying is a slippery slope for other types of anxiety. Perhaps you started worrying about meeting new people once again. Then you did everything you could to keep from interacting with them, to reduce your anxiety. You forgot that exposure is the antidote; it's like an inoculation. To both neutralize the worrying and prevent a setback, be sure to apply exposure.

Regardless of the factors that contribute to a setback, your task is to learn from the experience so that the setback can be worthwhile. Yes, worthwhile. Think of the setbacks as an opportunity to move ahead, rather than look back and lament.

You may have already had a setback. What did you tell yourself? What did you learn from the setback? What made you vulnerable, and what did you do to become less vulnerable to future setbacks?

How Do You Deal with Setbacks? WORKSHEET

HABIT #5
Yes, You Can Get Back on Track After a Setback

Getting over a setback means going back to anxiety practices that worked for you before.
TRUE

Recommitting to the anxiety-reducing habits you've learned will help you move forward in your recovery.

It's always disappointing to feel like you're headed backward when you feel like you were making progress. Remember, this happens to everyone who is trying to grow and change old habits for new, positive habits. The most important thing is to get back on track and practice the habits you've learned that are helping to reduce your anxiety. Remind yourself that each day you need to:

- *Keep yourself from overreacting to your physical symptoms through interoceptive exposure.*
- *Observe the sensations, instead of overreacting and seeing them as a call for alarm and eventual panic.*
- *Keep yourself from doing too many things at once and worrying about them all at once.*
- *Deal with each situation independently by chunking your tasks.*
- *Keep yourself from becoming too tired or hungry.*
- *Pace yourself so you don't feel pressured to complete a task too quickly.*

HABIT #6
Learn to Practice Assertiveness

Being assertive reduces anxiety because it makes you feel in control.
TRUE

Assertiveness shifts you from passivity to action, which activates your left frontal lobe and its positive emotions and reduces anxiety. Overactivating your right frontal lobe induces passivity and anxiety.

Being assertive allows you to meet challenges by confronting them head-on, instead of reacting to them in a passive, defensive way, always bracing yourself for the next onslaught of stress and anxiety. Being assertive can mean different things for different people. If you're shy, for example, being socially assertive will be harder than it would be for people who aren't shy. This doesn't mean that you get a free pass from making an effort socially. Your goal might not include becoming the life of the party, but you certainly can learn to be more assertive than you are right now.

You're in the Driver's Seat of Your Life

By being assertive, you're in the driver's seat of your own life, instead of the passenger seat. You decide where to go and what you want to do, instead of reacting to what occurs. Here's where your frontal lobes can have control over the reactivity of your amygdala. And here's where your action-oriented left frontal lobe balances out the passive right frontal lobe. Along with this shift to your left frontal lobe comes its positive emotions, instead of the negative emotions associated with the right frontal lobe.

Rate Your Skill Strength

Staying in shape means practicing all the techniques on a regular basis. The more you practice them, the more they will become second nature to you. They will become the new habits that replace your old anxiety habits. At this point, you'll want to determine what part of the full repertoire of practices you have been weakest in developing so that you can shore that up. Use the following worksheet to rate where you are strong and where you are weak. Rank them by assigning a number #1 for the strongest and so on. Also write down your plan to improve that skill.

MARA GAINS CONFIDENCE THROUGH ASSERTIVENESS

Mara had suffered panic attacks in her late adolescence, but they faded away rather quickly. Recently, she had taken a new job with a supervisor who did not value his employees. Simultaneously, she went through a rough time with her boyfriend. He, too, was experiencing stress, but his method of dealing with it was to dump it on her.

Mara's panic attacks reemerged after arguments with him and then increased in intensity over the following weeks. But she then began to practice all the skills that you learned in this book. She enjoyed a reduction in her symptoms and was delighted to see her panic attacks fade away.

Two weeks later, she had a relapse. She felt like she had "gone back to square one." She had had a series of panic attacks after she and her boyfriend had more fights and now feared that she had lost all the gains she had made.

She realized that setbacks are common, especially if relapse-prevention skills are not practiced on a regular basis. She assumed that she was cured and had completely conquered anxiety and so stopped practicing her coping skills. She ignored her diet and stopped practicing breathing exercises. By the time she and her boyfriend had their latest fight, she was already feeling free-floating anxiety.

Mara realized that she'd become far too passive in her life and needed to become more assertive. This was especially true in her relationship with her boyfriend. She tended to spoil him, and he took advantage of the opportunity to assume the role of the most important person in their relationship.

Learning to be assertive with her boyfriend wasn't easy. He didn't like that Mara was changing. However, when he said, "You've changed," she thanked him for the compliment. Of course, she knew that he was really complaining. She continued to develop assertiveness by telling him that her "change" would be permanent and that she would no longer sacrifice her needs to take care of him. Mara also practiced assertiveness at work. She and her coworkers began to discuss common purposes and cultivated mutual respect with the supervisor.

Mara began to feel confident again. But, this time, she didn't slack off on her relapse-prevention plan. Although she did experience some bumps along the way, with occasional periods of anxiety, she put things into perspective, and, with the use of her coping skills, those bumps drifted by as inconsequential.

HABIT #7
Focus on Your Weakest Skill to Make All of You Strong

It's okay to have some weak coping skills because your strong skills will balance them out.

FALSE

To prevent relapse, it's wise to improve your weakest skills to make your recovery more durable.

After you complete the previous worksheet, note the skills you ranked the lowest. Focus on making them your strongest skills. Your first response might be: "Why not stay with the ones I like the best?" or possibly, "What I've done already is good enough!"

You want to increase your durability as part of your relapse-prevention plan. To promote durability, you'll need to shore up your weak areas by practicing them more often and not rely solely on your strong skills. Consider this: You're only as strong as your weakest link. If you transform your weakest links into your strongest, your current strongest will be your weakest.

While you're strengthening yourself, you need to take care of yourself at the same time. Self-soothing behaviors involve doing not only things that help you relax but also things that excite and activate you. If you fall into a mode of always trying to relax, you'll relapse by developing anxiety sensitivity. You'll be so focused on reducing anxiety that any anxiety will feel like too much.

Balance Activation and Relaxation

You need a balance between activation and relaxation, between your sympathetic and parasympathetic nervous systems. Your sympathetic nervous system gets you activated. It helps you get excited about positive things, such as watching a good movie, playing your favorite sport, or embarking on an adventure. Positive things bring a rush of excitement and activate the neurotransmitters dopamine, norepinephrine, and epinephrine (adrenaline).

Your parasympathetic nervous system helps calm you down. If you focus too much on one system and avoid the other, you can set yourself up for an imbalanced life and a relapse of anxiety. You need both excitement and relaxation to keep your life varied, enjoyable, and balanced. Self-soothing, therefore, involves excitement as well as relaxation.

See the Glass as Half-Full

Remember that the way you perceive your symptoms or any given situation can either stoke up anxiety or help you cope with the situation. Include developing positive meaning for each experience in your relapse-prevention plan. The meaning is framed by your automatic thoughts, assumptions, and core beliefs. Relapse prevention is strengthened by the consistent positive and constructive meaning that you give to your experiences.

MICHELLE SHIFTS TO A CONSTRUCTIVE BELIEF

Michelle had a tendency to view the world as a hostile place until she came to an anxiety class. She grew up in a hostile neighborhood in South Central Los Angeles, where gang slayings were not uncommon. Although she was fortunate to earn a scholarship to go away to college, she had a hard time trusting people at school. Years later, after suffering periods of anxiety punctuated by panic attacks, she needed help. She wanted to shed her hypervigilance about who she could trust and began cultivating the skills to apply positive meaning to her experiences.

As she worked through the exercises and practices in this book, a rift had developed between her colleagues at work. Her coworkers were taking sides, almost like rival gangs, and she felt they were asking her to choose one over the other. Images of gang rivalry in her old neighborhood engulfed her.

Because of her hard work on her anxiety, she was able to shift to a constructive belief that the rift was beneath her and that she could focus on the higher common denominator between the opposing groups of people. She refused to come down to their level of winners and losers. She told those trying to recruit her that she would be glad to help them find common ground with those that they opposed. As she took the high road without alienating herself from personal relationships with her peers, her anxiety subsided.

These Guidelines Can Help Prevent (or Minimize) a Setback

Relish challenges. One of the most positive core beliefs you can embrace is to relish challenges. The hunger for challenge can be vitalizing. Your ability to stay flexible and assign positive meaning to all your experiences will be critical for facing challenges. Consider each new experience as a manageable challenge that is within your capacity to meet. Your thinking should promote optimism and the belief that you are up to most challenges.

Soothe yourself. Be prepared to soothe yourself as you encounter stress or periods of anxiety in the face of difficult situations. This can go a long way toward making a stressful situation tolerable. Self-soothing does not involve babying yourself. It simply means that you help yourself feel at ease during stress by using the relaxation skills that you've learned: breathing, positive self-talk, imagery, and self-hypnosis. Mindfulness will be especially useful to help you focus your attention and relax at the same time.

Regulate your emotions. Being able to regulate your emotions does not mean tightly controlling them. You learned that rigid efforts to stamp out any semblance of anxiety leads to more anxiety. Success in regulating your emotions involves letting go of the compulsion to control them. You can promote positive emotions by doing things that make you feel good and relaxed. If you are intensely focused on a particularly challenging task, incorporate your coping techniques, while challenging yourself to lean into that task.

Make anxiety your friend. Remember that a little anxiety is expected and perfectly normal. Your success is based on your ability to manage and orchestrate anxiety to make it work for you. Make anxiety your friend. Don't run away from it. This means that you must eliminate avoidance behaviors. Resist reverting back to old avoidant behaviors by telling yourself, "I've been good at pushing myself, and now I need a break from all this exposure stuff."

Eliminate safety behaviors. As you remember from the chapter on exposure, even safety behaviors are fool's gold. On the surface, they appear to be good ways to decrease anxiety, but they actually contribute to anxiety. Therefore, you want your relapse-prevention plan to eliminate safety behaviors. Don't give yourself an easy way out because you fear encountering some anxiety.

Stick with your exposure exercises. Consider them long-term treatments for anxiety. You need a "maintenance dose" of exposure exercises over the long term to keep yourself habituated to the experiences that you once found anxiety-provoking. Regular exposure is the way to stay "in condition."

Seek out social support. Social support is a critical part of your relapse-prevention plan. Because you are human, key parts of your brain thrive on social contact. You'll need these systems fully activated. These systems comprise what has been called the "social brain." They were very much involved in your early bonding experiences with your parents. These regions of your brain, which include your orbital frontal cortex, are highly involved in the regulation of emotion. When you activate your social brain, you also activate the parts of your brain that regulate your emotions. You do this by maintaining your social support system.

Withdrawing from your social support system deactivates your social brain. Your orbital frontal cortex will then be less useful in regulating your emotions. Even though you might not feel like being with people when you are anxious, social contact is still good for you. Think of it as "social medicine." Make sure that your relapse-prevention plan includes a regular dose of social medicine.

PETE LEARNS THE IMPORTANCE OF SOCIAL MEDICINE

An IT specialist in a huge law firm, Pete's job was to fix the firm's computer and network systems. Working in the office were more than fifty lawyers and seventy support personnel, who at times made Pete feel intimidated. He managed to keep himself insulated from social contact by minimizing small talk to focus solely on the computer systems. He had only one friend in the office, another IT person. Unfortunately, because much of the firm's work centered around real estate law, during the mortgage home loan bust, 20 percent of the office staff was laid off, including Pete's friend. His work load doubled, as did his anxiety level.

Always a worrier, Pete's anxiety was spurred to new heights. He found himself extremely sensitive to even an inkling of displeasure from the staff members. Because he had no friends to bounce things off of, those worries were like runaway trains. Initially, he resisted getting help because it meant joining group therapy and dealing with people. He didn't want to do it because he thought it would make his condition worse. But in addition to learning how to deal with anxiety, he would have an opportunity to practice social skills.

Pete's first few weeks in the group helped him rein in his anxiety and dampen some of his worrying. But he was quiet and only spoke to the therapist after the class, once the others had gone. It was obvious that he wanted social contact, because he stayed after group and wanted to make small talk. His therapist convinced him to arrive early and practice talking to his peers. She stressed that it was important for his long-term relapse-prevention plan to develop these small-talk skills at work. Expanding on these skills was important for his social medicine.

He dropped out of the group after about two months, explaining that he'd gotten what he needed. Three months later he returned, complaining that he had relapsed. He had continued with all of the anxiety-reduction skills but the social medicine. He said that he "got lazy," and it was "too much work" to make an effort socially. He essentially fell back into his comfort zone.

Pete's anxiety level spiked when the firm hit yet another financial crisis and more people were laid off. Staff members were getting irritable, and, when their computers broke down, they sometimes took their frustration out on him. Because Pete's relationships with many of them were dormant, he had no one to talk to, and his worrying once again intensified.

His return to the group presented an opportunity to emphasize how important social medicine is to a relapse-prevention plan. He began to practice his small-talk skills with peers, and soon the small talk became the gateway to deeper conversations. His desire for friendships spilled over into work. During the next financial crisis at work, the social medicine aspect of his relapse-prevention plan helped provide shock absorbers for the bumpy ride.

HABIT #8
Create Your Relapse-Prevention Plan

A relapse-prevention plan gives you the foundation you need to keep your anxiety recovery on track, no matter what happens.
TRUE

Your relapse-prevention plan can help ensure that you continue to move forward even when life gets challenging.

A holistic approach to anxiety recovery that includes many facets from a healthy diet to relaxation skills ensures better health and overall well-being and prevents setbacks. Your relapse-prevention plan should include many facets. Use the worksheet on the next page (154) to make sure that you adhere to each facet. As you continue to work on your relapse-prevention plan, remember that life itself is a challenge. And that's a good thing! Challenges make life interesting, exciting, and eventful. Face your challenges head-on, so that you can feel proud of yourself. Embrace those challenges, and, as a consequence, your anxiety will fade away.

In the date section of the worksheet, write down the date each week to ensure that you are staying on top of each aspect of your anxiety management. Use the blank spaces in the Domain column to write in specific parts of your unique monitoring plan. For example, if going to church or doing yoga is part of it, write it down. The important thing is to monitor all the facets of your plan so that you don't leave anything out.

Relapse-Prevention Monitoring WORKSHEET

	DATE	DATE	DATE	DATE	DATE	DATE
DIET						
BREATHING						
THINKING SKILLS						
EXPOSURES						
SOCIAL MEDICINE						
INTEROCEPTIVE EXPOSURE						
RELAXATION SKILLS						

	DATE	DATE	DATE	DATE	DATE	DATE
DIET						
BREATHING						
THINKING SKILLS						
EXPOSURES						
SOCIAL MEDICINE						
INTEROCEPTIVE EXPOSURE						
RELAXATION SKILLS						

MAKE IT A HABIT

Keep the worksheet handy and make copies so you can see it at home and work. Practice the habits that you've learned in this book and integrate them into your daily routine. If you feel like you've had a setback, let yourself off the hook and then recommit to the practices you've learned. When you make these practices a habit to overcome your anxiety, you'll be amazed at how much better you feel.

INDEX

A

abdominal breathing, 47, 48–49, 73, 124

abuse, 20

adrenocorticotropic hormone (ACTH), 28

aerobic exercise, 52–53

agoraphobia, 94, 105

alcohol use, 136

amino acids, 34–35

amygdala, 27, 28, 29, 67, 73, 104

anxiety and anxiety disorders

causes of, 18–20

examples of people experiencing, 13, 23, 66, 75, 83, 92, 117, 137, 139, 152

habits to help your overcome. See Habits

impact of, 7, 12

method of measuring the severity of, 23–25

necessity of *some*, 12

prevalence of, 7

types of, 14–16

worksheet identifying your type of, 17

anxiety sensitivity, 116–117, 148

anxiety triggers, identifying, 138

assertiveness, 146–147

assumptions, adopting anxiety-reducing, 82–83

Ativan, 8, 105

attachment relationships, 18, 20

automatic physical sensations, 119

automatic thoughts, 77–81, 119

autonomic nervous system, 27, 56

avoidance and avoidance behaviors, 92–98

anxiety sensitivity and, 116

avoiding, 104, 141

becoming bad habits, 95

dating occurrence of, 101

defined, 94

examples of, 92, 94, 105–106

forms of, 94

identifying types of, 96–101

making anxiety worse, 92

observation of, 107

questionnaire on, 93

replacing with exposure, 93

setbacks and, 151

B

Bandura, Albert, 120

Barlow, David, 117

beliefs

based on reality instead of how you feel, 72–73

restructuring negative core, 84–89

biological factors, 18, 19

biopsychosocial perspective, 7–8, 18, 19

black-and-white terms, thinking in, 18, 19, 20

bodily sensations. *See* Physical sensations

Body Tension Exercise, 128

brain-based practices, 7

brain-boosting foods, 42

brain, the. *See also* Frontal lobes (executive brain)

anatomy of, 27

diet and, 34

exercise and, 53

the gut and, 34

making new neural connections in, 26

mindfulness meditation and, 65, 67

synapses between neurons in, 26

thinking errors and, 73

breath(ing)

abdominal, 48–49, 73, 124

Holding Your Breath Exercise, 127

hyperventilation, 46, 47

Over-Breathing Exercise, 126

overbreathing/ hyperventilation, 46, 47, 125, 126

rhythmically, 58

self-hypnosis and, 63

stopping fight-or-flight response with proper, 4747

breathing difficulties, 15, 21

bridge phobia, 109

B vitamins, 39, 42

C

calcium, 41, 42

calmness, 55–69

diet and, 34, 35, 41

exercise and, 53

parasympathatic nervous system and, 56–57

The Seven Principles of Relaxation, 58–59

through meditation, 64–67

through prayer, 64

through self-hypnosis, 62–63

through visualization, 60–61

carbohydrates, 36, 37

catastrophizing, 19, 78

cerebral cortex, 27

challenges, 150, 153

chocolate, dark, 43

coffee, 43

cognitive behavioral therapy (CBT), 74

cognitive restructuring, 74

cold sweat, 15

complex carbohydrates, 36

concentration, difficulty with, 14

coping skills

about, 123–124

exercises, 126–131

focus on weakest, after setbacks, 148

forming new habits with, 123

identifying, 122

rating your strength in, 146

tracking your progress in, 125

core beliefs, 84–89

cultivating and constructing new, 88

example of person with negative, 89

formation of, 84

negative, 84-85

refuting old, 86-87

that increase your anxiety, 85

that serve you, examples of, 87

cortical-releasing factor (CRF), 28

cortisol, 28, 40

the critic (core belief), 85

D

depression, 8, 15, 39

dietary habits

amino acids and, 34-35

balanced meals, 36-37

calcium, magnesium, and potassium intake, 41

eating healthy fats and brain boosting nutrients, 38-39

impact on anxiety, 34

minimizing anxiety flare-ups with good, 136

water intake, 40

dizziness, 15, 46, 130, 131

dopamine, 34, 35, 39, 43, 148

driving, anxiety about, 23

drugs, avoiding, 136

dry mouth, 46, 119

E

either/or thinking, 77-78

emotional flexibility, 95

emotional reasoning, 78

emotional regulation, 150

endorphins, 53

epinephrine, 26, 27, 28, 35, 120, 148

escape behaviors, 94, 96-97

evidence-based practices, 7

exaggerating risk, 78

experiences, relabeling, 29, 59, 67, 75-76

exposure/exposure exercises

amygdala and repeated, 104

charting your progress of, 112-113

examples of people using, 106, 109, 111, 139

identifying short-term and long-term goals for, 110

identifying your avoidance behaviors and, 96-103

imagined, 108, 109, 111, 112

real-life, 108, 109, 110, 111, 138

replacing avoidance with, 93

sticking with, 151

extroceptive fear, 119

F

faint, feeling, 15, 21

fatigue, 14, 21, 39, 50

fats, eating healthy, 38

fear(s). *See also* Exposure/ exposure exercises

amygdala and, 27

avoidant behaviors and, 92, 94

of driving, 23, 105, 109

escape behaviors and, 96-97

exercise on examining, 102-103

extroceptive, 119

of flying, 105-106

interoceptive, 119

not avoiding real-life exposure to your, 138

of your physical sensations, 116-117

fermented foods, 35

fight-or-flight response, 28, 29, 47, 57, 120

flushed face, 15, 21

4-7-8 Breathwork, 48

free-floating anxiety, 14, 66, 92, 139

frontal lobes (executive brain), 27, 29, 59, 67, 73, 74, 75, 105-106, 136, 146

fruits and vegetables, 36, 37

G

GABA (gamma-aminobutyric acid), 26, 27, 34, 35

Gawain, Shakti, 61

generalized anxiety disorder (GAD), 14, 50, 66

genetics, 18, 20

green tea, 43

gut health, 34-35

H

habits

avoidant behaviors becoming bad, 95

brain-based explanation for formation of, 26

dietary, 34-43

doing what you don't want to do in order to change, 123

efforts for creating new, 26, 28

related to avoidant behaviors, 96-103

related to breathing, 46-51

related to exercise, 52-53

related to facing your fears, 96-113

related to physical sensations, 114-132

related to setbacks and relapses, 136-155

related to stretching, 50-51

related to your thoughts, 70-89

headaches, 39

Head Between Your Legs Exercise, 131

hemispheres, brain, 27, 67

higher consciousness, moving from self-awareness to, 69

higher power, 69

hippocampus, 27, 120

Holding Your Breath Exercise, 127

hydration, 40, 136

hyperventilation, 46 , 47, 125, 126

hypothalamus-pituitary-adrenal axis (HPA), 27, 29

I

imagery

self-hypnosis and, 62

visualization and, 60-61

imagined exposure, 108, 109, 111, 112

indigestion, 15, 23

interoceptive exposure exercises, 119, 125-131, 132, 147

interoceptive fear, 119

in vivo exposure, 108, 109, 110, 111, 112

"in vivo" exposure, 108

irritability, 14, 23, 39

L

labeling your experiences and emotions, 29, 59, 67, 75–76

left frontal lobe, 27, 59, 67, 74, 75, 105–106, 146

L-glutamine, 34, 35

lightheadedness, 15, 21, 46, 126, 131, 136

lobes, of the brain. *See* Frontal lobes (executive brain)

L-tryptophan, 35

M

magnesium, 41, 42

mantras, 58, 64

medical problems, side effects of, 20

medications, anti-anxiety, 8, 89

meditation, 57, 58, 64–67, 69

Mediterranean diet, 36

mental sluggishness, 39

mindfulness meditation, 57, 65, 66, 67, 73, 106, 150

movement and exercise, 52–53

multitasking, 136, 137

multivitamins, 42

muscle tension, 14, 21, 50, 52

muscle tingling/weakness, 39

mutitasking, avoiding, 136

N

nausea, 15, 21, 24

negative assumptions, 83

negative automatic thoughts/self-talk, 72, 79, 80

negative core beliefs, 84–86

negative emotions, 27

negative thoughts, 31

nervousness, 15, 21, 39

neurochemistry, 18, 136

neuroplasticity, 7, 26, 67, 73. *See also* Habits

neurotransmitters, 26, 27, 28, 34, 35, 39, 43, 148

nonjudgmental attitude, 59, 65, 66

norepinephrine, 27, 28, 35, 148

numbness, 15, 21, 46

O

observation, 59, 107

omega-3 fatty acids, 38

omega-3 supplement, 42

oribital frontal cortex, 29, 151

Over-Breathing Exercise, 126

overestimating risk, 78

overgeneralizing, 78

P

panic attacks

automatic thoughts and, 79

breathing and, 46

breathing/hyperventilation and, 46, 47

interoceptive exposure exercises and, 132

people experiencing, 89, 105, 137, 139, 147

panic disorder (PD)

assessment of physical sensations with, 120

hyperventilation and, 47

occurring with other anxiety disorders, 15

symptoms of, 15

parasympathetic nervous system, 6, 27, 47, 56–57, 148

parental influence, 20

Paxil, 8

the perfectionist (core belief), 85

peripheral nervous system, 27

pessimism, 19, 72

pessimism/pessimists, 89

the pessimist (core belief), 85

phobias, 16, 109

physical exercise, 52–53

physical sensations, 114–132

accepting and observing your, 118, 120

acknowledging and observing, 118

assessing your automatic, 121

biological aspect of anxiety and, 19

coping skills for, 122–131

fearing, 116–117

gut health and, 35

identifying your coping skills for, 122

learning to be more comfortable with, 119–122

panic disorder and, 15

"point focus," 58

positive assumptions, 82–83

positive self-talk, 116, 119, 124, 138

posture, relaxed, 59

potassium, 41, 42

potassium/potassium deficiency, 41

pounding/racing heart, 15

prayer, 57, 64, 69

prebiotic foods, 35

prefrontal cortex, 67

present moment, focused attention on the, 58

probiotic foods, 35

processed foods, 34

procrastination, 94, 99

progressive relaxation, 57

protein, 34, 36, 37

Prozac, 8

psychological factors/causes, 18, 19

psychosis, 39

Q

quiet environment, 59

R

rapid breathing, 46

rapid heartbeat, 17, 19, 120, 121, 126, 136

reality testing, 72–73, 74

real-life exposure, 108–109, 110, 111, 138

relapses and setbacks, 134–155

assertiveness/self-confidence and, 146–147

creating a relapse-prevention plan for, 153–154

example of person experiencing, 147

INDEX

focusing on your weakest coping skills for, 148-149

getting back on track after, 145

guidelines helping to prevent, 150-151

identifying your anxiety triggers to avoid, 138-140

overreacting to, 142-143

positive and constructive meaning given to experiences and, 149

realistic responses to, 143

self-care and, 136-137

relaxation, breathing practices for, 47, 48-49. See also Calmness

relaxation response, 47, 56-57

relax, inability to, 15

respiratory alkalosis, 46

restlessness, 14, 21

right frontal lobe, 27, 29, 74, 75, 105, 146

S

safety behaviors, 94, 100, 151

selective serotonin reuptake inhibitors (SSRIs), 8

self-care, 136-137

self-confidence, 120, 147

self-fulfilling prophesy, 85

self-hypnosis, 57, 62-63

self-soothing behaviors, 148, 150

self-talk (automatic thoughts), 77-81, 104, 106, 150

Serenity Prayer, 69

serotonin, 26, 34, 35, 36

serotonin-rich foods, 43

setbacks. See Relapses and setbacks

Seven Principles of Relaxation, 57, 58-59

shakiness, 15, 21, 136

Shaking Your Head Exercise, 130

sleep, 42, 136

social anxiety, 43

social anxiety disorder (SAD), 16, 34

social factors/aspect, 18, 19

social medicine, 151, 152

social phobia, 16, 119

social support, 137, 151

Staring Exercise, 129

stress, 38, 48, 64, 65, 72, 136, 150

stressful core beliefs, 84, 87

stretching exercises, 50-51

SUDS (Subjective Units of Distress Scale), 23-25, 102, 109, 110, 112-113, 125

SUDS Exposure worksheet, 113

sympathetic nervous system, 6, 27, 28, 47, 50, 56, 57, 58, 148

symptom clusters, 17

symptoms of anxiety. See also Physical sensations

assessing severity of, 22

associated with panic attack, 46

examples, 13

of generalized anxiety disorder (GAD), 14

measuring the severity of your, 22

not experiencing *all* symptoms of, 14

of panic disorder, 15

of phobias, 16

related to B-vitamin deficiencies, 39

of social anxiety disorder (SAD), 16

of social phobia, 16

worksheets on, 17, 21

T

theanine, 43

thinking errors, 72-73, 74, 79, 89, 136

thinking styles, 20

thoughts

changing your automatic, 77-81

cognitive restructuring and, 74

positive assumptions, 82-83

restructuring negative core beliefs and, 84-89

thinking errors, 72-73

tingling, 15, 21, 46

traumatic experiences, 20

trembling hands, 15, 21

V

Valium, 8

vegetables and fruits, 36, 37

verbal labeling, 75

the victim (core belief), 85

visualization, 57, 60-61

Vitamin B, 39, 42

Vitamin C, 38, 42

vitamin supplements, 42

W

walking, 52, 53

water intake, 43

Weil, Andrew, 48

worksheets

on anxiety symptoms, 21

assessing severity of your symptoms, 22

on automatic thoughts, 81

Avoidance Questionnaire, 93

charting your progress with balanced meals, 37

on coping skills, 126-131

on core beliefs, 87

to determine your anxiety type, 17

identifying avoidance behaviors, 97-101

noting cues that trigger your anxiety, 140

Relapse-Prevention Monitoring, 154

relaxation monitoring, 68

on setbacks, 144

on symptom severity, 22, 25

In Vivo Exposure, 110

on your physical sensations, 121

worrying, 14, 20, 21, 144, 152

Y

yoga, 51, 57, 59

Quarto.com

© 2025 Quarto Publishing Group USA Inc.

First Published in 2025 by Fair Winds Press, an imprint of The Quarto Group, 100 Cummings Center, Suite 265-D, Beverly, MA 01915, USA.
T (978) 282-9590 F (978) 283-2742

All rights reserved. No part of this book may be reproduced in any form without written permission of the copyright owners. All images in this book have been reproduced with the knowledge and prior consent of the artists concerned, and no responsibility is accepted by producer, publisher, or printer for any infringement of copyright or otherwise, arising from the contents of this publication. Every effort has been made to ensure that credits accurately comply with the information supplied. We apologize for any inaccuracies that may have occurred and will resolve inaccurate or missing information in a subsequent reprinting of the book.

Fair Winds Press titles are also available at discount for retail, wholesale, promotional, and bulk purchase. For details, contact the Special Sales Manager by email at specialsales@quarto.com or by mail at The Quarto Group, Attn: Special Sales Manager, 100 Cummings Center, Suite 265-D, Beverly, MA 01915, USA.

29 28 27 26 25   1 2 3 4 5

ISBN: 978-0-7603-9720-6

Digital edition published in 2025
eISBN: 978-0-7603-9721-3

Library of Congress Cataloging-in-Publication Data available
The content in this book previously appeared in
The Heal Your Anxiety Workbook (Fair Winds Press 2009)
by John B. Arden, PhD.

Design and illustrations: Timothy Samara

Printed in China

The information in this book is for educational purposes only.
It is not intended to replace the advice of a physician or medical practitioner. Please see your health-care provider before beginning any new health program.